D1038728

THE LAST WORD

ABOUT *EDUCATION WEEK* & EDITORIAL PROJECTS IN EDUCATION

EPE   EDUCATION WEEK

Editorial Projects in Education, or EPE, is an independent, nonprofit organization based in Bethesda, Maryland. EPE's primary mission is to help raise the level of understanding and discourse among professionals and the public on important issues in American education. Since 1981, EPE has published *Education Week,* American education's newspaper of record. *Education Week* keeps educators, policymakers, and interested others abreast of important news on preschool through grade 12 education from the local, state, and national levels. EPE also publishes *Teacher Magazine* and highly regarded annual special reports on a range of issues, including technology in schools, graduation rates and policy, and the progress of education reform in the fifty states and the District of Columbia. In addition, EPE runs the comprehensive education-news and information Web site www.edweek.org, and Agent K-12, a print and online job-recruiting service for educators.

Education Week Press, the books division of EPE, was launched in 2002 and has published titles such as *Cutting Through the Hype: A Taxpayer's Guide to School Reforms,* by Jane L. David and Larry Cuban; and *Win-Win Labor-Management Collaboration in Education,* by Linda Kaboolian and Paul Sutherland.

For essential information on all things education, please visit EPE at www.edweek.org.

EDUCATION WEEK

THE LAST WORD

THE BEST COMMENTARY AND CONTROVERSY IN AMERICAN EDUCATION

FOREWORD BY JAY MATHEWS

Commentaries selected by
MARY-ELLEN PHELPS DEILY
AND VERONIKA HERMAN BROMBERG

BICENTENNIAL
1807
WILEY
2007
BICENTENNIAL

John Wiley & Sons, Inc.

Copyright © 2007 by Editorial Projects in Education, Inc. All rights reserved.

Published by Jossey-Bass
A Wiley Imprint
989 Market Street, San Francisco, CA 94103-1741   www.josseybass.com

No part of this publication may be reproduced, stored in a retrieval system, or transmitted in any form or by any means, electronic, mechanical, photocopying, recording, scanning, or otherwise, except as permitted under Section 107 or 108 of the 1976 United States Copyright Act, without either the prior written permission of the publisher, or authorization through payment of the appropriate per-copy fee to the Copyright Clearance Center, Inc., 222 Rosewood Drive, Danvers, MA 01923, 978-750-8400, fax 978-646-8600, or on the Web at www.copyright.com. Requests to the publisher for permission should be addressed to the Permissions Department, John Wiley & Sons, Inc., 111 River Street, Hoboken, NJ 07030, 201-748-6011, fax 201-748-6008, or online at www.wiley.com/go/permissions.

Limit of Liability/Disclaimer of Warranty: While the publisher and author have used their best efforts in preparing this book, they make no representations or warranties with respect to the accuracy or completeness of the contents of this book and specifically disclaim any implied warranties of merchantability or fitness for a particular purpose. No warranty may be created or extended by sales representatives or written sales materials. The advice and strategies contained herein may not be suitable for your situation. You should consult with a professional where appropriate. Neither the publisher nor author shall be liable for any loss of profit or any other commercial damages, including but not limited to special, incidental, consequential, or other damages.

Jossey-Bass books and products are available through most bookstores. To contact Jossey-Bass directly call our Customer Care Department within the U.S. at 800-956-7739, outside the U.S. at 317-572-3986, or fax 317-572-4002.

Jossey-Bass also publishes its books in a variety of electronic formats. Some content that appears in print may not be available in electronic books.

Library of Congress Cataloging-in-Publication Data

The last word : the best commentary and controversy in American education/ editors of EducationWeek ; foreword by Jay Mathews.—1st ed.
     p. cm.—(Jossey-Bass education series)
  ISBN 978-0-7879-9606-2 (pbk.)
  1. Education—United States. I. Education week.
  LA217.2.L37 2007
  370.973—dc22   2007003999

Printed in the United States of America
FIRST EDITION
PB Printing   10 9 8 7 6 5 4 3 2 1

[CONTENTS]

PART NINE: INSPIRING LEADERSHIP

[F O R E W O R D]

Here we are, in the cable television news era, forced to accept the fact that discourse on public issues comes at us in blasts of rhetoric from politically connected experts in TV studios who are encouraged to be rude, not clear. Even in my allegedly more thoughtful business, newspapering, opinion pages have room for only short, acidic columns that rarely tell us all we want to know.

So it is a relief to open up this volume, *The Last Word,* and find that some of the brightest and most provocative thinkers in American education have been given enough space to make their points calmly and completely. Are the editors of *Education Week* old-fashioned? Good. We need a publication that provides on a regular basis deep and sprightly analyses of what ails our schools, and on how to fix them.

Putting so many of the finest pieces from twenty-five years of *Education Week*'s Commentaries into book form will help save readers like me from the messy habit of tearing out the latest *Ed Week* pieces and creating large, jumbled piles of them on our desks. Many of us need a way to understand the daily blizzard of rumors, e-mails, blogs, and press releases about American schools. These pieces are lighthouses marking where things really are.

The Commentaries are organized by subject matter. We can compare, for instance, Alfie Kohn's research-rich assault on the emphasis we put on tests ("Confusing Harder with Better") with E. D. Hirsch Jr.'s equally knowledgeable defense of testing done well ("The Tests We Need"). We get three able researchers (Marc Dean Millot, Paul T. Hill, and Robin Lake) making the case for charter schools in "Charter Schools: Escape or Reform?" while in "Make Public Schools More Like Private" the argument is turned on its head by a talented union leader (Adam Urbanski) who wants to make regular public schools more like charter and private schools.

I like the personal essays that make large points out of vivid memories of the classroom, such as Howard Good's ode to the AP English teacher who took a chance on a student not considered qualified for AP ("Epitaph for an English Teacher"), and James Delisle's take on a relative's remark that he was just too smart to become a teacher ("'Too Smart to Be a Teacher'").

My favorites in this collection are the Commentaries that knock you sideways with a thought so daring and ideologically incorrect that you have to read the thing right away and then talk to your friends about it. A splendid example is Saul Cooperman's very recent and well-titled "Increase Class Size—and Pay Teachers More." Not only did I read Cooperman's piece when it came out in *Education Week* in 2005, I also stole it. A few weeks after it ran, a story under my byline appeared in the *Washington Post* based entirely on Cooperman's wild but in some ways practical idea. I gave *Education Week* and Cooperman credit for the idea, but readers of this book are under no such obligation. Take whatever you like here and adopt it as your own. Your friends, like mine, will think you are much more clever than you actually are. What's wrong with that?

[JAY MATHEWS]

Jay Mathews is an education reporter and columnist for the *Washington Post* and a contributing editor at *Newsweek*. He has written three books about American high schools, including *Supertest: How the International Baccalaureate Can Strengthen Our Schools* (Open Court, 2005), coauthored with Ian Hill. He is also on the board of Editorial Projects in Education.

[PREFACE]

This book was a labor of love for many people, most notably a few lucky editors at *Education Week* who had the privilege of selecting the Commentaries that appear here. Still, choosing the essays was no easy task.

Since September 1981, *Education Week* has prided itself on being "American education's newspaper of record." Published by the nonprofit Editorial Projects in Education, *Education Week* was launched as a completely nonpartisan, independent newspaper covering elementary and secondary education exclusively. In keeping with that nonpartisan ethos, *Education Week*'s founders decided to forgo running their own editorials and instead created Commentary, an opinion section composed entirely of essays from outside contributors in the K-12 field and other observers of education. Over the years Commentary has evolved into something of an intellectual water cooler for the education community, a place where provocative and cutting-edge ideas can be shared in a thoughtful way.

The writers who have contributed to Commentary—which runs at the back of *Education Week,* hence this book's title, *The Last Word*—have included teachers, principals, school superintendents, policymakers, activists, and politicians. Their views have spanned the gamut—left, right, center, and impossible to pin down. They have addressed an impressive array of topics: racial discrimination, teacher preparation, school leadership, choice and charters, federal policy, and technology and education, to name just a few.

When the idea of a "best of Commentary" book first came up, it seemed fitting to present it in the context of *Education Week*'s twenty-fifth anniversary. Our goal was to pull together a representative array of Commentaries addressing critical topics facing schools today. It took more than a year of carefully sifting through the *Education Week* archives and engaging in countless conversations to winnow down the list of selected essays. Initially, *Education*

Week's editors planned on selecting twenty-five Commentaries for this anthology, one for each year of *Education Week*'s history. But limiting the list to twenty-five quickly became impossible, so we expanded. When we finally closed the list it was because we simply had to stop; needless to say, the finalist pieces that almost made it into this book were wonderful as well.

The writers whose Commentaries are collected in this book are, if not household names, important figures in their individual fields. But it was not their celebrity that attracted us—it was the power of the questions they raised and the issues they explored. When former teacher Jane Dimyan-Ehrenfeld writes, "Without exception, the best conversations I've had with any of the elementary school students I've taught have always been the ones I'm not really supposed to be having," how can you not want to know more? And when historian and scholar John Hope Franklin talks about "substandard schools, ill-paid teachers, poor equipment, students without equal opportunity, and educational programs that are pointless and fruitless," it seems imperative to listen.

It took a dedicated group at *Education Week* to assemble this book. Communications director Veronika Herman Bromberg and I worked closely together, and assistant Commentary editor Anne Das and associate design director Gina Tomko made key contributions. Commentary editor Sandy Reeves also offered helpful insights on particular pieces. Finally, this book is not the work of *Education Week* alone. When Jossey-Bass announced its interest in copublishing the book, *The Last Word* took a leap forward, and the input from the people at Jossey-Bass—right down to the book's title—has contributed greatly to the finished product.

It is the hope of everyone at *Education Week* that *The Last Word* will stimulate the kind of thought and conversation that Commentary has inspired for twenty-five years. In short, we hope you find this book as enriching as we have found the process of putting it together.

[**MARY-ELLEN PHELPS DEILY**]

Editorial Director
Education Week Press
October 27, 2006

Mary-Ellen Phelps Deily is editorial director of Education Week Press. Previously, she served as an assistant managing editor at *Education Week*, where she directed coverage of federal and state government policy and special education.

[PART ONE]

THE ART OF TEACHING

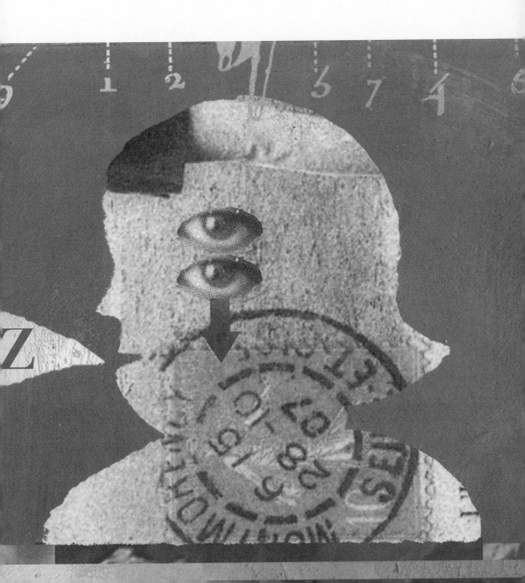

It has been more than six years since Harry Thompson, my fondly remembered Advanced Placement English teacher, died. During that time my long-held conviction that all high school kids need a Mr. Thompson in their lives to nurture and guide them has only grown stronger. But so have my doubts that they will find one. Teachers today may be too busy struggling to meet the demand for higher test scores to give kids the kind of encouragement Mr. Thompson gave me. I cannot conceive of a greater educational tragedy. For each kid whose talent goes unrecognized or undeveloped we're all irrevocably deprived and diminished.—HG

PUBLISHED OCTOBER 18, 2000

EPITAPH FOR AN ENGLISH TEACHER

[HOWARD GOOD]

He wasn't the most brilliant or stimulating teacher I ever had, just the most influential. His name was Harry Thompson. He taught me Advanced Placement English in 12th grade at John F. Kennedy High School—a class that, strictly speaking, I wasn't prepared for and shouldn't have been allowed to take. That was more than 30 years ago, but I still remember Mr. Thompson with a kind of awe.

Why? It isn't because he was physically impressive. He was a little pear-shaped man with a prematurely bald head that made him look a lot older than he was—only 37 at the time, if my math is correct. And it isn't because he was a flamboyant showman who entertained us with anecdotes and impersonations as he taught. His classroom style was actually rather drab. No, I remember him for the simple reason that he was sympathetic and encouraging to me when so many other teachers would have been the exact opposite.

I ended up in Advanced Placement English not because of my grades, which were mediocre at best, but because of my big mouth. The class had previously been confined to outstanding students who had followed an accelerated academic track since junior high. Average students like me were exiled to slower, lower-level English classes. I argued that this was elitist. During the political and social turmoil of the late 1960s, the argument must have carried a certain weight. The English department let me in.

And almost immediately I imploded. Although I harbored ambitions of one day becoming a professional writer, with my name on book covers and idolatrous readers at my feet, I hadn't yet mastered the basics of writing a critical essay. On the first major assignment—a paper on Arthur Miller's play *Death of a Salesman*—I got an ominous "See me" scrawled in red across the top. While the rest of the class trooped off to fifth-period lunch, I stayed behind. Sitting on the corner of his desk, Mr. Thompson dissected my paper with harrowing precision, pointing out lapses in interpretation, documentation, and even hyphenation. He suggested that perhaps I hadn't put enough effort into the assignment. The truth was worse. I had worked long and hard on the paper. It wasn't lack of effort but sheer ineptitude that accounted for all the mistakes. As he went on reciting my paper's shortcomings, I began to cry tears of frustration and shame.

I had had some teachers earlier in my school career who would have turned cruelly sarcastic at that moment. I had had others who would have remained indifferent. Not Mr. Thompson. He stopped in mid-sentence, the expression on his face alternating between surprise and concern. He didn't know me well. He didn't know about my literary ambitions. But he made it his business to find out. He became the first adult, beside my parents, to ever show any real interest in me. Over the next year I brought him my awful poems, and he lent me good books. He encouraged my writing, nurtured my imagination, and protected my dreams. I was just an average student, but he gave me the confidence to be more.

Mr. Thompson can be an inspiring example to all of us who are responsible in one way or another for educating the young—school board members, administrators, faculty, and staff. The educational community gives regular lip service to the notion that "every child can learn."

It is time—in fact, long past time—to put this notion into practice. Mr. Thompson demonstrated how.

First, be sympathetic to those in your keeping. You may have become accustomed to the sight of youngsters struggling with the rigors of growing up, but this is the first time through for them.

Second, never assume that a student is just average. Every student possesses the ability to excel at something worthwhile, whether drawing, science, or friendship. Third, grades count, but sincerity of effort counts too. Fourth and last, the opportunity to teach is ever present—seize it as often as you can.

Harry Thompson died this past summer of a heart attack. His body lay unclaimed in the hospital for several days. He had never married. He had no children. His only surviving relative was an older brother who was sick himself and couldn't get there right away.

But before you decide that Mr. Thompson suffered a tragic end, there is something else you should know. The week he died he received as a gift a copy of my newest book. I might never have written it or any of my five previous books if he hadn't gathered me up all those years ago. He made a positive difference in at least one child's life. So can you.

Howard Good is coordinator of the journalism program at the State University of New York at New Paltz and author of 13 books, the latest being *Mis-Education in Schools: Beyond the Slogans and Double Talk* (Rowman & Littlefield Education, 2007). He served for six years on the school board in Highland, New York, including three as president.

Today, in our era of artificial accountability, we worry if teachers are "highly qualified" instead of asking the more important question: "Are they highly effective?" Some effectiveness is measured by strong student performance on tests that measure the three R's. However, the most important element in teacher effectiveness lies someplace deeper, someplace less accessible to direct measurement; for unless a teacher inspires students to become fair, compassionate, ardent participants in our ever-changing world, their educations will remain incomplete and hollow. Now more than ever our kids need teachers who are smart enough to recognize this truth.—JRD

PUBLISHED SEPTEMBER 13, 1995

"TOO SMART TO BE A TEACHER"

[JAMES R. DELISLE]

When I was five years old and in the first grade, Sister Patricia Ann asked me to help her teach my 36 classmates their consonants. Later in the year, while we were learning to tell time, Sister asked me once again to help out. I could count to 60 by both ones and fives, a skill especially useful in that earlier era when clocks had hands and faces, not digital readouts.

At the end of first grade I announced to my parents that I wanted to become a teacher. They didn't say much. I said the same thing again in second grade, and fourth grade, and especially eighth grade (when Mr. Sheppard, my first guy teacher, was my hero). It was then, at my eighth-grade graduation party, that Uncle Ray took me aside to offer some of the advice he was so prone to give.

"Jim," he said, "you don't really want to be a teacher. There's no money in it. Besides," he added, "boys don't become teachers, girls do."

"But Uncle Ray, I had a man teacher this year!"

He just sighed, shook his head, and laying his hand on my right shoulder, added his final comment: "Jim, you're too smart to be a teacher."

Today I am what Uncle Ray admonished me not to become: a teacher, albeit a heavily credentialed one—B.S., M.Ed., Ph.D.—but a teacher nonetheless. Working in both a college of education and a suburban middle school, I have attempted to do what Sister Patricia told me I could do so well: teach others without making them feel bad that I knew some things they didn't.

I enjoy my jobs immensely, as do most of my colleagues, which is why it bothers me so much that the same advice I received from Uncle Ray more than 30 years ago is still being given to wannabe teachers today. The difference is, the people who now most often say "You're too smart to be a teacher" are not well-intentioned yet out-of-touch relatives, but rather educators themselves who want to take away from others the dream they themselves had sought: to become a teacher.

Why is this? Why do so many individuals who work daily with young people discourage the most capable ones from entering the field of education? I can't imagine it's the low pay (except in South Dakota, salaries are pretty decent— and on the rise). It can't be the feeling that one cannot make a difference— every teacher has virtually dozens of stories of student success. And it can't be a lack of camaraderie—teachers' lounges are hotbeds of lives in motion.

Perhaps this aversion to recommending a career in education is due to a perception that educators aren't as respected as they once were, by either students or the public. Maybe it's because teachers' unions have become so powerful that the personal voice of one teacher is stifled by the din of the many, leaving individual accomplishments secondary in importance to collective bargaining. Or maybe it's the restrictions placed upon the art of teaching by the too-numerous proficiency tests and reforms mandated by out-of-touch legislators and "experts" who dictate from afar how we should do our jobs.

Even though I don't know all the causes of dissatisfaction, I do know this: in both my university and in many K-12 schools, a career in education is considered the lowest of the low in terms of professions that matter. And the people one would assume to be most enthusiastic about what they do—educators themselves—are often the field's most vocal opponents. In the now-familiar words of Pogo, "We have met the enemy, and he is us."

To be sure, educating today's youths in our virtual-reality culture is a tough task. We compete with Big Bird (at least until the Contract with America makes him extinct) and Power Rangers. We vie for the attention of kids raised on Nintendo and Prodigy. We try to teach 30 students at a time as the individuals they are, knowing full well that those at the extremes, the very brightest and the educationally neediest, are somehow missing out on the full measure of what they need to succeed.

Yet these realities are little different from the interferences that plagued past generations, when the introduction of rock and roll, radio, TV, and even the backyard swimming hole all provided new nirvanas for students to explore. Though more complex in nature, today's distractions from academics still share some common ground: each appeals to children who are active, friend-conscious, and more interested in having fun than in learning math facts. Times may change, and the kids may become more superficially sophisticated, but a deeper look reveals what should be obvious: students need caring and intelligent adults to teach them as much as they ever did.

I'm sure some readers will find me naive, perhaps believing that those bifocals I've just begun wearing were fitted with rose-colored lenses. They may even tell me Uncle Ray was right—that a real professional would look for a higher-status job than classroom teaching, or that teaching at any level is a career relegated to those who choose to settle for something less than they are capable of doing (the "Those who can, do; those who can't, teach" syndrome). They'll suggest that teaching should be just a steppingstone to something more meaningful—like administration or personnel management.

In small but gnawing ways, comments like these send two messages to prospective teachers: first, that the further removed from children they become, the more important their job in education is; and second, that becoming a career teacher is professionally stifling. Both messages are wrong, for to assert that teachers must remove themselves from the classroom to feel professionally fulfilled is akin to asking Whoopi Goldberg to direct "Oklahoma!" in order to round out her resume.

Of the many naysayers in our profession I kindly ask a favor: resign or retire or retrain or do whatever it takes to reignite the idealism that brought you into the field in the first place. Leave education until such time that you once again believe anything is possible in the life of a child—drugs, poverty, or emotional bankruptcy notwithstanding. If educators do not see their ability to make a meaningful difference for a child who believes in the inevitability of his own defeat, they are taking up valuable space in front of a classroom—space that can and should be occupied by an optimist who takes the role of teacher seriously—and assumes it with pride.

And while they're at it, these same teachers who complain that education is not a worthwhile career should realize that by discouraging able young people from becoming teachers, they not only downplay dreams but also demean themselves and a noble profession. It's easy to bemoan one's lot in life, but guess what? No one is forcing teachers to remain teachers against their will. In the words of former Chrysler Corporation chairman Lee Iacocca, "You've got to lead, follow, or get out of the way." So if education is as bad as some teachers say it is, then those unhappy pessimists should stop frustrating themselves and exit the corps.

The longer I teach—it's been 18 years now—the more firmly I believe that the finest teachers are born, not made. That all of the teacher education courses and national accreditation standards in the world can't create an educator out of someone who just doesn't wholeheartedly want to be working with children's minds, hopes, and dreams. I also believe that many prospective teachers knew when they were six, just as I did in Sister Patricia's class, that teaching was the only job worth having. To those bright young people who want to enter the profession that has been so good to many of us—education—I say "good choice!" My advice to them is not, "You're too smart to be a teacher," but rather, "You're too smart not to be one."

That single affirmation, if made by every educator alive who believes in its truth, could be the greatest impetus ever in our collective move to reform the profession.

James R. Delisle is a distinguished professor of education at Kent State University and a part-time middle school teacher in Twinsburg, Ohio. He is also author of more than 250 articles and 14 books, including *Gifted Kids' Survival Guide: A Teen Handbook*, coauthored with Judy Galbraith (Free Spirit, 1996). His work has appeared in such popular media outlets as the *New York Times* and the *Washington Post* and on National Public Radio and *The Oprah Show*. Delisle is president of Growing Good Kids, Inc., an educational consulting company based in Kent, Ohio.

Since this essay was written, Carnegie Corporation of New York and the Annenberg Foundation have joined together to support the Learning Network, a forum for higher education institutions dedicated to reforming teacher education. Through the network, 30 additional reform-minded institutions have been invited to participate in the Teachers for a New Era effort. In addition, the final report of the Teaching Commission (Spring 2006) notes that the commission "remains impressed by the work of Carnegie Corporation of New York, whose Teachers for a New Era initiative is changing the way teachers are trained. . . . Carnegie is committed to measuring the results of these reforms by eventually looking at the actual learning gains made by students taught by these programs' graduates."—VG

PUBLISHED NOVEMBER 10, 2004

NO MORE SILVER BULLETS

Let's Fix Teacher Education

[VARTAN GREGORIAN]

As autumn comes into focus each year, American education experiences an unseemly spectacle. I'm referring to the annual scramble of school districts across America to recruit teachers who will educate our nation's children. Paradoxically, teacher shortages and the emergency recruitment of teachers—which in recent years has included "headhunters" roaming foreign lands with hiring bonuses clutched in their hands—highlight both the importance of teachers and their role in our society and, at the same time, lead to the conclusion that it is relatively easy to fill these jobs. The granting of so-called emergency teaching licenses on a routine basis to uninitiated and untrained recruits is a short-term solution to what is shaping up to be a long-term disaster. For in the next decade, our nation's schools will need to hire millions of teachers ready to move a generation of young Americans into the knowledge-based economy. American colleges and universities are not prepared to meet the challenge—and they must be.

How is it possible that the United States, which claims to have three-fourths of the world's finest universities—and boasts 1,300 schools of education—has in recent years not only lacked qualified teachers but also had to venture beyond its own borders to find them? For answers, we may look to our own economic rules of supply and demand. After all, the nation never seems to lack for lawyers, doctors, and architects, but always seems to have a "Teacher Vacancy" sign blinking outside the schoolhouse door. Why hasn't teaching flourished, following the path of other professions? A century ago, law, medicine, and school teaching were all considered to be vocations. All of them became professions, but the status of teaching never rose very high.

The other professions gained high status by developing prestigious training schools and rigorous certification for entrance and advancement. They are vigilant against substandard institutions and training programs. Also, accountants, engineers, and other valued professionals are respected for their *special* knowledge. Their careers give them authority, autonomy, and independence to make important decisions. It goes unquestioned that professionals must receive adequate support, the latest technology, and work environments conducive to efficiency and creativity. As to compensation, as we know, society usually rewards them generously. Teaching clearly falls short on all of these professional markers. In this connection, we should heed the warning of Louis V. Gerstner Jr., former chairman of IBM and currently chairman of the Teaching Commission (of which I am a member), who reminds us, "We [as a nation] will not continue to lead if we persist in viewing teaching—the profession that makes all other professions possible—as a second-rate occupation."

We can no longer close our eyes to the problem of America's schools of education and the pitiful job most of them do in preparing our teachers.

We are all fooling ourselves if we think that the past 20 years of standards-based education reform will ever result in our nation's children being provided with the quality education they need without a dramatic parallel reform effort in the training of teachers. My bookshelves are sagging under studies that say the quality of teaching is the most important variable affecting student achievement, and survey after survey proves that Americans overwhelmingly believe that improving teaching is one of the most important strategies for improving schools. In an age of global competition, which spans every sphere of human endeavor, a society that settles for anything less than providing high-quality education for all its citizens is going down a dangerous path. It is nonsense to talk about raising standards for students when their teachers often do not meet the same high standards. It's not surprising that mediocre teachers produce mediocre students.

Presidents of America's colleges and universities—where virtually all of our nation's teachers have earned degrees—must step up to the challenge and forcefully, both individually and collectively, discredit the prevailing view that teaching is just another job that anyone with a couple of weeks of intensive training can perform. Each must make it clear that teaching institutions must *prepare teachers who are proficient in the fields they will be teaching, well-versed in the latest theories and practices of pedagogy, skilled in technology, and professionally mentored with solid classroom experience.* This is the gold standard of teacher education that must be put in place, and no institution or university worth its reputation can settle for less. Once and for all, we must retire George Bernard Shaw's tired old maxim, "He who can, does. He who cannot, teaches." On the contrary, we must remind our fellow citizens that teachers are arguably the most critical "doers" in our society, for they bear the awesome moral, social, and historical responsibility of creating our nation's future through the education of our children.

What, then, should be the starting point in any teacher education reform effort? It seems to me that our nation's schools of education, given the huge responsibility they bear, must not only be equal in caliber to their sister institutions comprising the American campus but must also occupy a central role in the university—conditions that, alas, they do not meet. And while they are looked upon as "separate but unequal," they are nevertheless also regarded as a fiscal resource for universities, providing a steady source of unrestricted income and held up as a shining example of public service, since they provide teachers to educate the nation's young. (This is a particularly important role for state universities' schools of education, since they can point to a direct benefit to the state in producing homegrown teachers.) All of this comes at the expense of schools of education: since so few of them have endowments of their own, they frequently find themselves doing what's expedient rather than what's right for themselves and their students, meaning they resort to increasing enrollments and lowering standards in order to raise income. Is it any wonder, then, that these schools so often end up being the choice of those most unprepared to succeed in higher education, most undecided about what to do with their lives and careers?

Isolated and marginalized, with separate faculties and separate activities, schools of education dwell in the shadow of their favored university siblings, the schools of arts and sciences. This situation cannot continue without causing lasting damage, not only to schools of education and their students but also to the universities themselves, and to their reputations.

The public should send a loud and clear message to university presidents, faculties, and governing boards that they have no choice but to make teacher education a central preoccupation of their respective institutions. Indeed, as education leaders, they must make this issue their *personal* central preoccupation. They must either integrate their schools of education with the schools of arts and sciences, along with the rest of the university—bring them into the intellectual mainstream—or shut them down. What they cannot do is continue to subject the schools of education to "benign neglect." This should make eminent sense to educators, who certainly know that without quality teaching, the education of our children is not a realizable goal. Without teachers drawn to their profession by a real love of teaching and learning and a true commitment to the challenge of transmitting knowledge and wisdom to the next generation, the great ideas that infuse us with energy, the ideals that make us strive to live better lives, the dreams that built our democracy—indeed, the very DNA of our nation—may be lost.

We are all paying a high price for the poor state of our schools of education—and that includes American higher education itself. Unprepared teachers produce unprepared students, who then show up at the doors of colleges and universities needing remedial work in order to participate at higher education levels. This set of circumstances means failure and disappointment for young people who depend on our educational system to equip them to succeed, but can also be counted in literal dollars and cents. That's a costly equation that should be recalculated at its source: excellent teachers preparing students who are ready to take on the challenges of postsecondary education is good business, not only for teachers and students but also for the universities themselves. It's in their own self-interest to have students who can keep up with their schoolwork from the moment they set foot in their first college class.

Despite the many fine education reform efforts of the past 20 years and the national commitment to learning that the federal No Child Left Behind Act appears to embody, teachers have not been provided with the necessary training and support to carry out these mandates. As the National Commission on Teaching and America's Future observed, in the absence of quality teaching, "all the directives and proclamations are simply so much fairy dust." In that connection, I am personally committed to removing once and for all the excuse that teachers are not well compensated and do not enjoy the status of other professionals because they are not well prepared. I believe that if we really want to improve learning, then we must improve teaching. I refuse to blame our teachers for their professional shortcomings while overlooking the failures of the higher education institutions that are responsible for educating and training them. We have a sacred responsibility to the young men and women who step forward to declare, "I want to be a teacher." Our part is to help them become *good* teachers—*excellent* teachers—and when they do, to reward them accordingly.

As for that sacred responsibility, let me suggest that most universities should thank God that their alumni who are now teachers have not brought a class-action suit against them for letting their schools of education send teachers out into the world who are not prepared or trained to keep up with the constant need to increase their subject-matter expertise and pedagogical skills, or to achieve higher levels of professional development in order to cope with the explosion of knowledge and information that characterizes 21st-century life and learning. Not to mention the fact that they also have to be able to interpret, manage, and successfully interact with the myriad regulations, administrative structures, and legalities that govern K-12 education.

The time is right for intervention, and Carnegie Corporation of New York has embraced this extraordinary opportunity with a multimillion-dollar, five-year reform effort designed to strengthen K-12 teaching through the creation of a new model of teacher education. The initiative Teachers for a New Era represents the corporation's commitment to translating two decades of research and public discussion into substantive teacher education reform. The leaders of each of the 11 institutions of higher education selected to participate in the initiative have agreed to organize their teacher education reform efforts around three fundamental principles:

- Research evidence must ultimately demonstrate whether children have experienced learning gains as a result of the work of teachers who are graduates of the teacher-preparation program.

- Full engagement of arts and sciences faculty is required in the education of prospective teachers, as well as ongoing collaboration between the faculties of a university's school of arts and sciences and its school of education.

- Viewing education as an academically taught clinical practice is required, one which includes close cooperation between colleges of education and participating schools, master teachers as clinical faculty in colleges of education, and two-year residencies for beginning teachers.

The 11 institutions participating in Teachers for a New Era were invited to work with the Carnegie Corporation on this initiative not just for their excellence but for their potential as catalysts for improvement, as incubators of change. Because they are such a diverse and eclectic group—large and small, East and West Coast, public and private, Ivy League and state institutions—they can demonstrate to the hundreds of institutions like them that there are no excuses, and that well-supported, well-endowed schools fully integrated into the vibrant learning community that is a university can succeed in making a long-term educational impact. We hope they can provide viable models for others to emulate as well as prove that American schools of education can—and *will*—bury forever the excuse that "we just can't fix the problem."

And the timing of this initiative is critical. The participants in Teachers for a New Era have, in effect, agreed to make the case for university-based teacher education at a pivotal moment when school districts, in desperate search of that silver bullet, are increasingly looking outside the university to develop teacher-preparation alternatives. So the gauntlet has been flung down: Are America's universities up to the task of providing American students with well-trained, enthusiastic, skilled, and knowledgeable teachers, or are they not?

Although it is my hope that Teachers for a New Era will contribute significantly to the redesign of schools of teacher education, I am acutely aware that no single reform initiative will get the job done. Every hope inevitably has a corollary. Mine is that Teachers for a New Era will serve as a catalyst for many other worthy teacher education reform efforts. What we cannot accomplish alone we can accomplish through cooperation, collaboration, and creating models that can be replicated.

Together, the leaders of America's institutions of higher education can ensure that the millions of teachers that this nation will need in the next decade or so will be superbly prepared, highly motivated, highly valued, and eager to begin their journey in this noblest of noble professions. Quite simply, what is riding on the success of our combined efforts is the future of every child in America—and for that, I say, failure is not an option.

Vartan Gregorian is president of Carnegie Corporation of New York in New York City. Prior to joining Carnegie Corporation in 1997, Gregorian served for nine years as president of Brown University and for eight years as president of the New York Public Library. In 1998 he was awarded the National Humanities Medal, and in 2004, the Presidential Medal of Freedom, the nation's highest civilian award.

Reducing class size requires a huge expenditure of dollars. One would think the evidence would be overwhelming that the smaller the class size the more children would learn; the evidence is not there. When will we realize that most teachers teach a class of 20 exactly the same as they teach a class of 30? Use the money to pay teachers more: attract better teachers and retain them. That, not lowering class size by five or ten children, will make the difference.—SC

PUBLISHED NOVEMBER 2, 2005

INCREASE CLASS SIZE—AND PAY TEACHERS MORE

[SAUL COOPERMAN]

Back in 1982, as New Jersey's commissioner of education, I made several recommendations to then-Governor Thomas H. Kean concerning teachers. These ideas, all of which the governor embraced, stirred controversy, but also put our state on the cutting edge of school reform. The alternate route to certification was a rigorous system designed to open the doors of teaching to bright and talented graduates of liberal arts colleges. Dramatic increases in beginning teachers' salaries were to create a ripple effect that would raise all teaching salaries. Changes in staff development turned the emphasis from single in-service days and college courses to solving the practical problems teachers face. With access to excellent research, teachers could apply the information where it counted, in the classroom. And a program honoring the state's outstanding teachers was instituted to provide the recognition that fuels motivation and builds professional identity.

These ideas were all implemented between 1983 and 1990. They were important because they recognized, in a practical way, what we all pay lip service to: the notion that teachers are extremely important. With this in mind, I have a suggestion that would significantly upgrade the quality of teachers in our country, reduce persistent teacher shortages, increase student learning, and not cost any more money. What's the catch? It would require establishing class size at from 30 to 35 students in all grades except K-3.

What I am suggesting is heresy to most people, because everybody seems to love smaller classes. Teachers want them; parents believe the smaller, the better; and the public generally has bought in. Unions love small classes because the smaller the class size, the more teachers there are, and the more union dues. And to the graduate schools of education, having more teachers for smaller classes is a cash cow.

Of course the research has been decidedly mixed for many years. For every study showing that class size makes a difference, another study says it does not. Recently the University of London's Institute of Education traced 21,000 British children over three years of schooling. The researchers concluded that, for the most part, class size seemed to matter little to the students' progress in English, math, and science.

Undaunted by such findings, the smaller-is-better advocates feel that children will receive more attention as the pupil-to-teacher ratio is reduced, and therefore will learn more. And if class size is 20 instead of 30, teachers feel there will be a greater opportunity to individualize their lessons, fewer children might be discipline problems, and less time will be needed to grade papers.

But the question remains: Are smaller classes good public policy? Most teachers teach 20 children exactly the same way they would teach 30; there is no real change in most teachers' approach to how they teach, despite fluctuations in class size. Individualization is more intention than reality.

And there couldn't be a more costly approach than small class size in the eternal attempt to improve student learning. For example, for a school of 1,000 students with a class size of 30, we would need 33 teachers. For the same 1,000 students, if the class size were 20, we would need 50 teachers. If the average salary for our teachers were $50,000, the payroll for the 33 teachers would be $1.65 million. For 50 teachers, the payroll increases to $2.5 million, an increase of $850,000—more than 51 percent. Add the cost of new classrooms necessary to house the extra 17 teachers, and the yearly expense to maintain the additional space (heat, light, janitorial service, insurance, and so forth), and the result is clear: a *tremendous* commitment of dollars. In the name of "quality education," school administrators continue to recommend this approach, and school boards seldom question whether it is worth the money.

There is an alternative to the lower-is-better panacea that is not complicated at all, but as I've indicated, it is heretical to most educators and parents alike. Increase class size and use the money saved to pay teachers more. Take the additional $850,000 that would be used to reduce class size and use it to increase teachers' salaries.

So if we raised class size and salaries in our hypothetical school of 1,000 students, we would have 33 teachers making an average of $75,757, not $50,000. What would this get us? We would need fewer teachers, so the shortage in any school or district would decrease significantly, or perhaps even be eliminated. But this is only one reason for trying the approach. The primary reason is that the higher pay would attract a much better pool of candidates.

Brighter teachers are the best hope we have of increasing student performance. Grover J. "Russ" Whitehurst, director of the federal Institute of Education Sciences, has said that "the most robust finding in current research literature is the effect of teacher verbal and cognitive ability on student achievement." So, the brighter the teacher, the better the chance for students to learn more. This needs to be repeated: *the brighter the teacher, the better the chance for students to learn more.* And thousands of very bright and able people would choose to teach if salaries were dramatically increased.

Would teachers' unions buy this plan? On a local school level, I think so, because unions first and foremost are made up of people who operate in their members' interest. And a 51 percent pay raise is certainly in a union member's interest! Would the local unions oppose the trade-off of increased class size for a pay raise of more than $25,000 per member? I doubt it. At the state level, however, unions might argue against such a proposal. As a practical matter, needing fewer teachers would mean fewer dues-paying members, with a loss of financial clout for the union's lobbying and political agendas.

What about the justifiable gripe that mediocre teachers would be rewarded equally with the outstanding ones? This concern is as valid today as it would be if boards of education implemented this approach. A solution is something that is long overdue in most districts, and the problem is not unique to my proposal.

While some districts have comprehensive and fair systems of supervision and evaluation for teachers, most do not. A majority of administrators and supervisors engage in what former General Electric CEO Jack Welch refers to as "superficial congeniality." The supervision is superficial, and evaluation results in almost every teacher's being recommended for the standard annual increase in salary. Yet there are many models of good supervisory and evaluation plans available that could be implemented. The only thing missing in most districts is the will to make supervision and evaluation the most important job of the administration. With more than 60 percent of every current-expense portion of the budget allocated to teachers' salaries and benefits, attention must be paid, whether or not my suggestion to raise salaries and class size is taken.

The forces supporting the status quo in any aspect of life are powerful, and education is no exception. Will educators and parents debate this proposal on the facts rather than emotion? Maybe. Facts are stubborn things, and if the debate on this proposal could be played out in the field of research rather than through anecdotal examples, change just might occur in hundreds of school districts.

Were that to happen, such districts would be able to demonstrate that they can hire more highly qualified teachers while at the same time reducing or eliminating teacher shortages—with students as the ultimate beneficiaries.

It can be done.

Saul Cooperman is former New Jersey state commissioner of education and currently chairman of the Academy for Teaching and Leadership in Far Hills, New Jersey. A former history teacher, high school principal, and superintendent of schools, Cooperman is author of *How Schools Really Work: Practical Advice for Parents from an Insider* (Catfeet Press, 1996).

PART TWO

EQUITY AND SOCIAL JUSTICE

I very much wish I could say that we have made great strides in the improvement of education since 1984. I cannot, for the simple reason that I do not see any significant improvement. Two examples will suffice. First, in the very important area of racial desegregation, we are moving in many places in the opposite direction. In many school districts there is a clear move in the direction of segregation. Second, in the federal legislation subsumed under the title "No Child Left Behind," the emphasis appears to be more on testing than on learning, with the result that students today appear to focus much more on achieving grades than on obtaining knowledge. Consequently, I am not greatly encouraged by developments in the educational enterprise since I addressed the problem in 1984.—JHF

PUBLISHED OCTOBER 31, 1984

"THE NATIONAL RESPONSIBILITY" FOR EQUALITY OF EDUCATIONAL OPPORTUNITY

[JOHN HOPE FRANKLIN]

This essay was adapted from remarks made by the author upon receiving the Jefferson Medal of the Council for Advancement and Support of Education in Washington, D.C., 1984.

The need to solve the problems of education in this country is as urgent today as it ever was. Whether one is talking about public or private education, lower or higher education, the need is critical. First, we lack sufficient material resources to provide the physical equipment and the teaching personnel that are required. In cities with gleaming skyscrapers and bustling industries, the schools are too frequently ramshackle, run-down, substandard accommodations unworthy of those who seek to learn within their walls. Second, we lack faith in the value of education, except in its most mundane application, and because of that our commitment to the general educational enterprise is less than enthusiastic. Finally, we seem to have no clear notion of where responsibility for education really resides—at the local, state, or national level—and we equivocate, vacillate, even speculate, about which level has the greater responsibility.

The question of responsibility was not always a problem in this country. The legislative bodies of colonial Massachusetts and Connecticut enacted laws in the 17th century requiring every town with 50 inhabitants or more to support a public school. If some did not comply, it was not because of lack of clarity in the legislation or lack of parental interest. Rather, it was because of extremely limited resources or because children were needed to work on family farms and in shops. It must have been extremely painful to parents and legislators to see their schools languish, for their commitment to education could hardly be questioned. "We in this country," said Jonathan Mitchell in the middle of the 17th century, "being far removed from the more cultivated parts of the world, had need to use utmost care and diligence to keep up learning."

During the early years of the independence movement, education remained a responsibility of local government, and the general commitment to education was greater than ever. Even before the War for Independence was over, new state constitutions, forged in the crucible of war, reiterated the importance of education and the need to spread it everywhere. These were among the earliest expressions of the desirability of viewing education in national terms. The Massachusetts Constitution of 1780 stated the matter eloquently: "Wisdom and knowledge, as well as virtue," it said, "diffused generally among the people and being necessary for the preservation of the rights and liberties," it was imperative that the government spread "the opportunities and advantages of education in various parts of the country and among the different orders of the people." The thinking that went into this statement—and indeed the statement itself—is as valid today as it was two centuries ago.

Unfortunately, the patriots had their inconsistencies and lapses in the field of education as in other areas. Consequently, they did not find it necessary to pay even lip service to such ideas as equal educational opportunity or universal education. Women were not included in the many expressions of solicitude about the general diffusion of knowledge. Afro-Americans, slave and free, simply could not have any educational opportunity that might lead to their enjoyment of the rights and privileges for which they also had fought during the War for Independence. Native Americans most assuredly were not in the educational plans of the states or the new national government.

These conditions, which deprived a considerable portion of the population of an opportunity to learn, reflected a flawed social and political orientation of the country generally. As a result, women would still be waging the battle for equality not only in education but in every aspect of life down to the twilight years of the 20th century. Black Americans would first seek to repeal the laws that held them in bondage and then would wage an uphill struggle against the numerous barriers placed in their way because of their race and color. For three centuries and more, Native Americans would seek to throw off the stigma of being aliens in their own land and then fight against the contention that they were unteachable, uncivilized savages.

As the nation grew in age and experience and as the people spread over the vast lands, many of them became more sensitive to the relationship of education to democratic institutions. They began also to work out justifications and strategies for the support of education on a national basis. They were keenly aware that the government, under the new Constitution, did not assume responsibility for education. Yet the new government had recognized its critical importance by including the provisions that had been made in the Ordinances of 1785 and 1787 for the maintenance of schools in every township and for the encouragement of education.

This sufficed, perhaps, until 1862, when the federal government committed itself much more specifically to some responsibility for education. That year, Senator Justin Morrill sponsored the bill setting aside certain public lands in each state for the benefit of education in the fields of agriculture and the mechanical arts.

Having committed itself to a major role in higher education, the federal government might have been expected logically to take another major step. It did not. Instead of providing resources from land or minerals for the support of secondary or elementary education, or both, it took a step much less bold, if somewhat innovative. In 1867, it established the United States Office of Education, which was charged with collecting "such statistics and facts as shall show the condition and progress of education in the several states and territories." The office published hundreds of monographs and reports between 1867 and its demise in 1980.

As the Office of Education made studies and issued reports, the states developed their own programs of education in any manner they wished. Since the federal government took no active role in policy decisions and gave virtually no support to the states, except to their land-grant colleges, the states did exactly as they pleased. Where racial segregation existed, they made no effort to equalize educational opportunities. In 1900, the per-capita cost of education in Adams County, Mississippi, was $22.25 for whites and a mere $2 for blacks. And during those years the matter was not an issue in any state or local political campaign and was surely of no concern to the federal government. Negroes themselves were rapidly losing through constitutional disenfranchisement what little political influence they once had. No president, no commissioner of education, no one highly placed in the federal establishment spoke out against these clear violations of the constitutional rights of several million American boys and girls who happened to be black. What was true of blacks was true of Native Americans and, in some cases, of females as well.

In the 20th century, wars and the media were nationalizing forces in American life that led to a degree of uniformity in some areas, such as tastes, tradition, and entertainment, but certainly not in all. In education, little uniformity exists. This is not to imply that a uniform curriculum is beneficial, but rather to suggest that uniformity of opportunity and some semblance of gratifying results may be desirable goals that are too seldom attained.

As far as opportunity is concerned, what is there in Arkansas, for instance, to match the Bronx High School of Science in New York or the North Carolina

School of Science and Mathematics? What is there in Montana or Georgia comparable to the Mark Twain School for gifted children in St. Louis? Are there no children in Arkansas who could profit from the two years of calculus those at the Bronx High School of Science receive? Are there no gifted children in Montana who could benefit from the excitement available to the students in the school for gifted children in St. Louis? What child in this country would not learn more if his or her school had a decent library, despite the fact that the president of the United States seemed proud of the fact that his school in Illinois had no such facility. The point is that there is no one, no apparatus, to monitor the common educational needs of American students. Consequently, some students receive an education with different attractive features or, indeed, with no attractive features.

Not only is there no equality of opportunity in education, there is also no equality of resources among school districts. Mississippi and North Dakota cannot build and equip their schools and compete successfully in the marketplace for teachers in the way that, say, New York and Pennsylvania can, for the simple reason that they do not have the resources. How tragic, therefore, if the brightest young boy or girl grows up in Mississippi or North Dakota with their limited educational opportunities, while less able children grow up in Westchester County, New York, and Bucks County, Pennsylvania, with every conceivable educational opportunity.

What is true about unequal opportunities from state to state is true within states and even within communities. Why should county schools provide a better educational opportunity than the city schools? Or vice versa? Why should a youngster living on one side of town be privileged to go to a better school than one living on the other side?

It has been argued with considerable force that one of our clear national responsibilities is to provide equal educational opportunities for disadvantaged children, which often means black children and white children below the poverty level. Of course such children need the support and protection of the strongest possible arm—the federal government. To deprive such children of the right to every educational opportunity available for any other child is to place insurmountable barriers in their way and sentence them to a life of continued disadvantage. But any child—white or black, rich or poor—who does not have access to the best education the nation can afford is disadvantaged and deserves the support and protection of his or her federal government.

When the Department of Health, Education, and Welfare (HEW) was established in 1953, it was a significant recognition by the federal government that it had an important, definable responsibility in the area of education. It was an unequivocal commitment to study, monitor, and, yes, to make available a considerable portion of its enormous resources in the effort to improve the quality of education and to equalize educational opportunities among the various segments of our society. Doubtless this sense of responsibility was quickened by the Supreme Court decision in *Brown* v. *Board of Education* in 1954, and also in the attempt to catch up with the Soviet Union in the post-Sputnik years. The year after the establishment of HEW, the federal government spent $355 million on public elementary and secondary schools. By 1978, the figure had increased to $6.5 billion. Without doubt, these dollars met an urgent need, and most school boards said, "Keep the dollars rolling in."

Shortly thereafter, the federal role in the educational process came under close scrutiny and, finally, bitter attack. The fight reached a climax during the debates over the proposal to establish a federal Education Department with Cabinet status. At that point, all of the pent-up hostility to "big government" control of local affairs was vented on the proposed department. There were already too many federal bureaucrats meddling in education, the opponents argued. Washington would merely ruin our quite satisfactory school systems, they insisted. The department would politicize educational programs in the worst possible way. How could anyone who sincerely believed in the American educational system countenance a federal department?

The new Education Department barely had time to organize itself before it became a storm center in the presidential campaign of 1980. With the incumbent president a staunch supporter and the Republican nominee a firm opponent, the lines were drawn. And when the new president appointed a former commissioner of education as his secretary of education, some concluded that his single assignment would be to preside over the dissolution of the Education Department. It was not long before the president, and perhaps even his secretary of education, saw in the department a marvelous opportunity to infuse the entire American educational enterprise not with badly needed resources or even welcome suggestions regarding reforms in the curriculum, but with strong advice about the importance of local control, merit pay for teachers, prayer in the schools, and placing a teacher in outer space. The department, whose days were numbered in 1981, is flourishing today as a strong political right arm of the Reagan Administration's "New Beginning" policies.

Intentionally, I have not addressed certain deplorable conditions in our schools: violence, drugs, assaults on teachers, strikes, hostility among school boards, administrative personnel, and teachers. I have preferred to give attention to the problem of the framework in which our schools must live or die. It seems to me that the best chance to get at the problems and solve at least some of them is to place them in a national context and impose on them a national responsibility. They cannot be solved on a local basis any more than they can be solved in a vacuum. They are so critically important to the future of this country that they deserve to be attacked with all the power and resources at our command. The talent, experience, and material resources needed for their solution can only be commanded by the nation as a whole, acting through its national agencies such as the federal government.

Nothing I have said should be interpreted as advocating a national system of education. That would not be in keeping with the spirit and tradition of this country. But substandard schools, ill-paid teachers, poor equipment, students without equal opportunity, and educational programs that are pointless and fruitless are not in keeping with the spirit and tradition of this country either. We need a total approach to these problems and their solution. That, in turn, requires the assumption of responsibility by all of us; and that means a national responsibility.

John Hope Franklin is James B. Duke Professor Emeritus of History and for seven years was professor of legal history in the Law School at Duke University. He is also the namesake of Duke's John Hope Franklin Center for Interdisciplinary and International Studies. In 1984, Franklin was presented with the Jefferson Medal of the Council for Advancement and Support of Education "for extraordinary contributions to American society."

The changes to the American population suggested in my essay have all come about, but the responses have been "sanitized" to make them more palatable: rather than the 128 racial combinations mentioned here, the census reports collapse them all into a single box for "persons of more than one race," although racial identity remains confusing. This box was checked by 4.3 million people, and more than 40 million "Hispanics" were double-counted as white because Hispanics are not a race. While a third of U.S. residents are something other than white, so are 45 percent of kids under five. These children are the future. Educators should be concerned that two-thirds of households have no children at all, that about half of our kids are cared for by a married couple, and that youth poverty remains at 17 percent while only 10 percent of people over 65 in the United States are poor. Why should this be?—HH

PUBLISHED SEPTEMBER 29, 1999

CENSUS 2000 IS COMING!

[HAROLD HODGKINSON]

The 1990 U.S. Census was easy. Public school students were classified as white, black, Native American, Asian/Pacific Islander, or "other," as far as their race was concerned. ("Hispanic" was not a race but an ethnic group, so Hispanics also had to pick a race.) So, only five races and one ethnic group were defined; these have been unchanged since 1977, when the boss of the Census, the White House Office of Management and Budget, issued Directive 15, outlining the racial and ethnic categories for the Census. Interestingly, in the first paragraph of that directive, one reads, "These categories have no scientific validity." If not scientific, what *are* they? Answer: one of the biggest public opinion polls ever—if you think you're black, you're black. Race is of the utmost importance historically and politically but is scientific nonsense. Earlier Census takers used diagrams of various lips, eyes, noses, and hair to decide what race a person was, which was even worse than having people decide for themselves. In Census 2000, all bets are off. For a decade, people of mixed ancestry have been lobbying for a Census that would describe everyone accurately. Project RACE, which stands for Reclassify All Children Equally, is one of a number of such organizations. A minimum of 3 million schoolchildren are racially mixed, and the actual number is probably triple that amount. In addition, 35 percent of U.S.-born Hispanics are marrying non-Hispanics, and 45 percent to 55 percent of U.S.-born Asians are marrying non-Asians, following a trend begun by Americans with European backgrounds. Only 15 percent of U.S. citizens of European extraction now represent, say, an Italian married to an Italian, a German to a German, or a Swiss to a Swiss. Yet in 1900, if a German married an Italian it was called miscegenation. (See *American Demographics,* December 1997.)

As a nation, we "melt" by marrying people of different racial, ethnic, and national origins. Yet "race" remains a major political force, even as the physical differences we associate with it are fading away through intermarriage. Today in America, the darkest fourth of the white population is darker than the lightest fourth of the black population.

Responding to these pressures, as well as to court decisions that have upheld the principle that children cannot be forced to choose between their mother's and their father's ancestry, the Federal Interagency Committee's final recommendations for the 2000 Census, issued in October 1997, suggested a major expansion in our definition of race and ethnicity: Black and African-American became two categories, because there are 3 million black Hispanics, mostly Caribbean, who do not consider themselves African; Asian became two more—Asian and Native Hawaiian/Pacific Islander (most Chinese do not consider themselves in the same category as Hawaiians); Indian became two more—American Indian and Alaskan native; plus white and "other," for eight categories.

However, the 1997 statement allows every American to select as many categories as he or she wishes. The simple checking of one of five boxes in the 1990 Census becomes a matrix of 8 × 8 in the 2000 Census, or *64 boxes*. If you allow Hispanic/non-Hispanic for all categories, the matrix becomes *128* boxes. (There is considerable pressure to add categories for the approximately 3 million people from the Middle East—1,000 mosques now exist in the United States—plus the 3 million Americans from the former Soviet Union. Both are as much an "ethnic group" as Hispanics, but this would push the combinations well into the stratosphere, if not outer space.)

William P. O'Hare, Kids Count coordinator at the Annie E. Casey Foundation, has suggested that this will be a data-collection nightmare for school administrators (no federal money for Title I, special education, school lunch, and so on, unless you include an analysis of your students by "race"), and even more so for policy analysts.

The young golf sensation Tiger Woods, for example, has claimed that he is a "Cablinasian," allowing him to check all four—Caucasian, black, Indian, and Asian—boxes. Fine. Next question: Does Tiger Woods count for four people with his four checks? Does each checked box equal exactly one-quarter of his ethnic heritage, and if so, by what logic? Can Tiger Woods be counted as black for affirmative action purposes and as white for housing and health surveys? What of the Hispanic child with a Mexican mother and a Cuban father—is that "mixed race"? (The odd answer is that a Hispanic couple, one from Cuba, one from Mexico, will be forced to choose only one nation of origin, while races can check as many as they wish in Census 2000.) How can you add all these boxes to get back to the individual who was split up in the first place? (Tiger Woods' four checks must "add up" to only one person.) If you just count all the boxes checked, the U.S. population could go from 280 million to 600 million. In addition, the black population could leap from 32 million to 50 million, or it could decline to 20 million, depending on how people perceive themselves, and how many cells they check.

For research purposes, it's clear that Census 2000 won't be compatible with the 1990 results. If you want to compare the growth of the black population from 1990 to 2000, the 1990 figure is easy, but what number should be used for 2000? All the people who checked *only* black? Should they be given more statistical weight than those who checked black along with other "races"? What happens to the valuable studies of the National Assessment of Educational Progress for various racial and ethnic groups through time? Are minority students going to college in greater numbers in 2000 than in 1990? Are federal and state programs and social services geared to certain racial and ethnic groups (for example, the Indian Health Services) going to the "right" people? All longitudinal studies of student performance through time, like the National Educational Longitudinal Survey and the Schools and Staffing Survey, will be in serious difficulty.

It is true that for most school districts, this new census requirement will not change things much, as 85 percent of America's 3,065 counties are still 90 percent or more white. Indeed, just 10 states—California, Texas, New York, Florida, Illinois, New Jersey, Arizona, New Mexico, Colorado, and Massachusetts—contain 90 percent of the country's Hispanic population, while 43 percent of Asian-Americans live in only three metropolitan areas: San Francisco, Los Angeles, and New York City.

But even in a county that is 0.5 percent black, 0.2 percent Hispanic, and 0.2 percent Asian (99 percent white), the 64- or 128-cell school survey will have to be filled out. And if the "diverse 1 percent" is 30 students, each of whom checks six (different) boxes out of the 128, the point should be made. Billions and billions of taxpayers' money will be allocated on the basis of these categories, yet no one has suggested that all the congressional legislation be modified to include these new categories or their combinations.

Most important, the human and fiscal cost of reporting to the federal government on the racial and ethnic diversity of every student in every school of every district of every state in the Union could easily triple, and the results could be much less useful for the educational enterprise, at all levels. (Student financial aid in America's colleges and universities will have to be given out in some very new and complex ways.)

Many others are salivating at this new complexity, especially business marketers who are hoping to discover many new niche markets within the gross totals available to the users of previous censuses. On questions of where to put that new bowling alley, the new ethnic restaurant, what languages to use in the new bank ATM machines, what kind of toothpaste Koreans will buy, and so on, Census 2000 may well become a bonanza. But for America's schools and colleges, the next Census may become a complex, ambiguous, and basically nonuseful tool, which schools will have to follow in providing district, state, or even federal information, or face the risk of losing federal money.

If the 2000 U.S. Census is to be as accurate a description of the American people as possible, a "mirror held up to nature," it is likely that the image will be so blurred as to be unrecognizable. And that may turn the country away from a concern solely with racial inequities and toward the ultimate problem: a 20 percent poverty rate among youths in the United States. Being black is no longer a universal handicap, as 20 percent of black households have a higher income than the white average.

Being born poor *is* a universal handicap, regardless of race or ethnicity. Many people are beginning to think of *economic* desegregation as a more productive way to a better society, and the confusion produced by the 2000 Census regarding race may only increase this new commitment, particularly regarding the economic inequities between city and suburb.

Harold Hodgkinson has served as director of the Center for Demographic Policy in Alexandria, Virginia, since 1987. He holds a doctorate from Harvard University and has received 12 honorary degrees. Mr. Hodgkinson was one of three Americans awarded the title of Distinguished Lecturer by the National Science Foundation in 1989. He is the author of 12 books, three of which have won national awards, and more than 200 articles.

It is difficult for anyone who is paying attention to the state of our nation's public schools not to be discouraged about the current state of affairs. Even as our nation becomes more diverse—no ethnic group will constitute a majority of the population by 2050, or put differently, whites will become a minority group—our nation's schools are becoming more segregated. This is particularly true in our nation's largest cities, where we have concentrated our poorest students in districts that are generally underfunded and that more often than not show little ability to meet their educational needs. Unlike 30 years ago, when there was at least some political will to address racial segregation, today we demonstrate tacit acceptance for the status quo as we mouth slogans such as "leave no child behind." For those who recognize that education will be the defining civil rights issue in the years ahead, the critical question is how long we will passively accept these conditions. How we respond to this question may very well determine what kind of nation we will be in the future.—PAN

PUBLISHED MAY 19, 2004

THE LEGACY OF "ALL DELIBERATE SPEED"

[PEDRO A. NOGUERA & ROBERT COHEN]

This Commentary was written to commemorate the 50th anniversary of the Brown decision. Coverage of the anniversary was underwritten by grants from the Ford and Rockefeller Foundations.

How should the nation commemorate the 50th anniversary of the U.S. Supreme Court's decision in *Brown* v. *Board of Education* of Topeka? We could celebrate this historic decision for outlawing apartheid in public education and establishing a precedent for ending racial segregation in other areas of American society. Or perhaps more realistically, we could reflect on the court's vagueness about enforcing this decision—its offering the odd term "all deliberate speed" in place of a real timetable for school desegregation. With this phrasing we can see that imprecision as the first of many evasions that even liberal whites made when it came to translating *Brown* into educational policy.

The legacy of this history of avoidance and delay has left our public schools so segregated (though on a de facto rather than a de jure basis) that there are good grounds for questioning whether there is much to celebrate on *Brown*'s 50th anniversary. New York City's public schools serve as an excellent example. At first glance, they appear to be among the most diverse in the world. Over 100 different languages and cultures are represented among the 1.1 million students, and over a third of those students are either foreign-born or the children of newly arrived immigrants.

But a closer look reveals that the ghost of Jim Crow lingers even amid this multicultural mosaic. More than 73 percent of the city's schools are virtually segregated. Approximately 900 schools have student populations that are 80 percent to 100 percent African American, Latino, or both. The schools are segregated by income as well as race. In the vast majority of these schools, more than 85 percent of the students qualify for free or reduced-priced lunches. Although over 40 percent of New Yorkers are white, only 15.3 percent of the students enrolled in the city's public schools are U.S.-born whites.

Much of America shares with New York this pattern of profound race and class isolation. Even the sites of some of the most famous victories for school desegregation, such as Central High School in Little Rock, Arkansas, have, because of white flight, resegregated. In the 1990s, the proportion of black students attending all-minority schools rose from 33 percent to 37 percent, and in the South the proportion of black students enrolled in white-majority schools plummeted from 44 percent to 33 percent. Disturbingly, Latinos, who now make up the fastest-growing ethnic group in the nation, are now more likely to be segregated than any other group.

Unlike 50 years ago, when there was a growing sense that racial integration was a moral goal worth pursuing, today that optimism has vanished, and segregation in our schools and elsewhere is accepted as an unavoidable feature of life in America.

The president's No Child Left Behind law contains no plan to support racial integration or to further equity among poor and affluent schools. Even Democrats and other liberal critics of this law have said nothing about its failure to deal with the persistence and expansion of de facto segregation in America's schools. Thus one way to truly honor *Brown* may be to challenge the left and right sides of the American educational debate to stop running away from the issue of school segregation.

A second way to commemorate *Brown* would be to honor those few school districts that are still trying to make school desegregation work, such as the 21 districts in the Minority Student Achievement Network. These districts have defied national trends and remain racially and socio-economically integrated. Though challenged by a variety of equity issues and a persistent achievement gap, such districts serve as an example of what might have been if we had had the leadership and resolve to realize the goals of *Brown*. Though far from perfect, such districts show us that one of the most important benefits of integration is the presence of middle-class parents who utilize their political clout to advocate for resources that benefit all students, and students who are better prepared to handle the challenges of living in a diverse society because of the education they received.

We can also honor *Brown* by revisiting the issue of integration in communities of color. Many black and Latino communities gave up on school integration long ago because of white resistance to busing. In many cases, desegregation also resulted in the closure of schools in black and brown communities and the loss of African American teachers. As a result of these unintended consequences of *Brown*, many communities of color are increasingly focusing on how to make our racially separate schools more equal. That focus has yielded a small number of successful, selective public schools that cater primarily to black and Latino students. Schools such as Frederick Douglass Academy in Harlem and the Young Women's Leadership School in Manhattan demonstrate that it is possible to create educational institutions that produce high levels of achievement for students of color in racially segregated settings, when adequate resources are provided.

The success of such schools also suggests that, for the time being, the best hope for many minority children may be to accept racial segregation and do what we can to create more high-quality segregated schools. While this may be the most pragmatic thing to do, we must also recognize how our sights have been lowered as we return to the unfulfilled "separate but equal" promise of *Plessy* v. *Ferguson,* the fatally flawed, segregationist U.S. Supreme Court decision that *Brown* overturned.

Throughout the country, the more common experience for students is to attend schools that are separate and unequal—schools that are well-equipped and cater to the children of the affluent, and schools that barely function and serve the poor, white and nonwhite. Throughout America, a majority of poor children attend schools where learning has been reduced to preparation for a standardized test, where failure and dropping out are accepted as the norm, and where overcrowding and disorder are common. Those who believe that integration remains a goal worth pursuing must recognize that no law can force middle-class whites to enroll their children in schools they seek to avoid, because they are either too black or simply too bad, for the sake of integration.

So perhaps the best way to honor *Brown* is to use it to recast the current debate over school reform. Let's stop seeing reform as an end in itself and start asking how improved schools in all communities can be used to attract multiracial student enrollments to those schools. And let's start demanding that *Brown*'s vision of integrated schools be addressed by politicians of both major parties. Unless we do so, our children, sitting in racially segregated classrooms, would be more than justified in thinking us hypocrites, pretending to celebrate a school integration decision that our nation has spent a half-century evading.

Pedro A. Noguera is a professor in the Steinhardt School of Education at New York University and director of the Metropolitan Center for Urban Education. He is author of *City Schools and the American Dream* (Teachers College Press, 2003), among other books. His most recent book is *Unfinished Business: Closing the Achievement Gap in Our Nation's Schools* (Jossey-Bass, 2006).

Robert Cohen is chair of the Department of Teaching and Learning in the Steinhardt School of Education at New York University. His publications include *The Free Speech Movement: Reflections on Berkeley in the Sixties* (coedited with Reginald E. Zelnik, University of California Press, 2002), *Dear Mrs. Roosevelt: Letters from Children of the Great Depression* (University of North Carolina Press, 2002), and *When the Old Left Was Young: Student Radicals and America's First Mass Student Movement, 1929–1941* (Oxford University Press, 1997).

As expected, this is a story without end. Issues related to being a white teacher educator in a multiracial society with a history of racism continue to challenge me. By continuing to accept the challenge, I am forced to rethink and refine my response to students, such as the one in a recent class who told me she "had never thought about race in terms of things like access to college." As for my daughter, her choir experience was integral to her ensuing college studies, including her senior thesis in African American history.—PMC

PUBLISHED JANUARY 26, 2005

RACISM EXPLAINED TO MY WHITE DAUGHTER

[PATRICIA M. COOPER]

My daughter, a college sophomore, joined her university's gospel choir this year. The choir was founded to celebrate African American culture. We are white. Beyond the joy of singing wonderful music, the benefits to my daughter of membership in the choir are obvious, from learning a lot about African American history to participating in deep discussions on such questions as whether nonbelievers have a right to sing Christian-themed lyrics. She's also getting firsthand experience as a nonmajority member of a group. All told, an opportunity hard to argue with.

Recently, however, the choir selected individual members to take on tour, and my daughter was not among them. As is her nature, she agonized over why. Was it her singing? She couldn't be sure, of course, but she thought she compared favorably to students who had been asked to go. Could it be her level of commitment? No, she was sure she had worked very hard to be a responsible group member. Eventually she got around to wondering if race had been a factor in who was selected. How could this be? Was it possible that the color of your skin made a difference after all?

Maybe, I told her. But maybe not. You'll never know unless you ask, I said. She said she couldn't. She didn't want to appear whiny, or worse, as if she felt entitled. I reminded her that blacks regularly confront not knowing whether they have been turned down, or out, or away because of their skin color. My daughter wasn't consoled. Well, what if it's true? I asked. I reminded her that she's pro-affirmative action, and that there are times when racial accommodations make sense for the good of the group, or the individual, or the goal. Still, no consolation. Finally, I joked that if the goal was to showcase a gospel choir, just how many blue-eyed blondes do you need? She didn't laugh.

I tried another tack. History. Not African American history, but mine.

There were many lessons I had to learn as a young white teacher working with black children and their families on Chicago's South Side. The lessons were different from what my daughter is trying to figure out, of course, as they are different again from what my education students, most of whom are white, are trying to learn as future teachers in New York City, where an overwhelming majority of children and their families do not look like them. The one common thread that runs across the years and the venues, however, is the need to acknowledge that being white in a conversation is not the same as being black. This doesn't mean one perspective always trumps the other. It only means that we've got to be unsparingly honest about what's at stake for both parties.

I told my daughter how devastated I was as a young kindergarten teacher on the South Side when a black mother demanded to know why her twin girls insisted that their hair would be like mine when they grew up, that is, very long, very blonde, and very straight. I, of course, protested immediately that I hadn't done a thing. She didn't look at all convinced. Next, I tried to play it down. All kindergarten girls want to look like their teachers, I said. At this she looked angry. I then stammered my way through a promise that I would try to be extra sensitive to the problem and see what I could do. She had barely gotten out the door when I began assuring myself that no one worked harder than I to be a colorblind teacher. My insides actually hurt with the unfairness of it all.

Twenty years later the *Nappy Hair* controversy erupted, wherein a white teacher was excoriated by black and Hispanic parents for reading her class an award-winning children's book. By then I had learned enough to know that the twins' mother had not only been right to be worried but also had a right to ask. She was trying to tell me that hair is a racialized issue in America. I had tried to tell her it wasn't. Finally, I had to accept that the twins' mother, who, by the way, was one of the first I knew to wear her hair in its natural style, knew more about being black than I did.

I also shared with my daughter my experience with another black mother in that same school. She had four children under the age of six, one of whom was in my class. Until family night I thought we were on good terms. Thinking she would appreciate the gesture, I reserved a large table for her, the kids, and me, and helped with the dinners as I chatted about large families. After the evening's events she sought me out in the lobby. Loudly and furiously, she first called me a "white bitch" in front of half the school. Then, screaming, she demanded to know what right I had to think she needed my help or to insult her for having so many children.

With this my daughter finally had something to laugh at, seeing the ridiculousness of the allegation in light of her 11 aunts and uncles, my siblings. She guessed, though, that it probably wasn't funny to me at the time. It wasn't. I was mortified and humiliated in front of my colleagues, the children, and the other parents. I was also deeply frustrated by the assumption of racism. Who better than I could anticipate any mother's need for help with four small children?

Of course my sense of injustice made me conveniently forget what I knew most people think about families with too many children in a row. How often after I left my Irish working-class neighborhood for college and graduate school had I been stunned by what perfect strangers would say upon learning of my six brothers and five sisters, let alone the three-bedroom Bronx apartment I invariably had to admit to? You wouldn't think that, on hearing such information, so many random people would automatically think to ask if my father could read. But trust me, there are too many. And before I learned to find them silly, I hated them.

So why was I so surprised when that young mother fought back against a perceived insult to her family? She was a young, black, single mother of four on welfare. I was her age, married, and working on my second master's. Though I still wish she had chosen another way to express her anger, the fact is that no matter what we had in common, there was more we did not. Did I think she didn't notice? Civil rights activist Myles Horton puts it this way in *The Long Haul: An Autobiography* (Teachers College Press, 1997):

> You're white, and black people can't say they are colorblind. Whites and white-controlled institutions always remind them that they're black, so you've got to recognize color. This doesn't mean you feel superior, it's just that you've got to recognize that you can never fully walk in other people's shoes. You can only be a summer soldier, and when the excitement is over, you can go back home. That doesn't mean that you don't have solidarity with black people and aren't accepted; it just means that you have a different role to play.

We have to keep thinking about the terms of the conversation, I told my daughter, if for no other reason than that, as Myles Horton suggests, we never take it for granted. This is something I never stop learning. I relayed to my daughter, for example, an incident from one of my education classes that centered around Ann Haas Dyson's *The Brothers and Sisters Learn to Write*. I asked the students, all of whom were white, why they thought the children in the book, all of whom were black, wrote stories steeped in popular culture. A perfectly pleasant, hard-working young woman responded quickly. "Well, what else would they write about?" she said. "They have no experiences."

No one challenged her. Disappointed, I asked the student, "What kind of experiences do white kids have to write about?"

"Oh, you know," she answered. "Ballet lessons. The violin. Things like that."

"You mean, all of the white kids you know take ballet lessons and play the violin?" I responded.

"Well, no," she said, "but I'm sure they do other things after school besides watch TV."

"Like black kids do" was the unspoken assumption. It was clear that it had not occurred to her that black kids, including black kids who write about popular culture, might have after-school lessons. Or that white kids might not. And it certainly never occurred to her that white kids thrive on popular culture too. Most important, she had yet to enter into a conversation where she might learn something worth knowing from black kids.

I asked my daughter if she was willing to quit the choir. No, she said. I was glad. I couldn't promise what it would all mean to her in the end, as I can't promise my white education students. I am only sure that, if she's willing, the experience won't be short on lessons learned.

A month later the choir director told my daughter that a place had opened up on the tour. Did she still want to go? She did.

Patricia M. Cooper is assistant professor in the Department of Teaching and Learning at New York University in New York City. She acknowledges her debt to Tahar Ben Jelloun, author of *Racism Explained to My Daughter* (New Press, 1999) for inspiring this essay's title.

PART THREE

TESTING WELL, TESTING FAIRLY

The more things change, the more they stay the same. In 1992, Albert Shanker challenged our country to develop world-class standards. Today, most teachers have neither clear standards nor curriculum nor aligned assessments to guide their instruction—Shanker would say they've been left high and dry. We continue with standards that vary from state to state, and performance expectations that are even more diverse. The concept of national standards has reemerged as a solution to reconciling these differences. The American Federation of Teachers (AFT) continues to be drawn toward a national system of standards, but we recognize the imperative of first establishing common terms and understandings about what this means.—Antonia Cortese, executive vice president of AFT

PUBLISHED JUNE 17, 1992

BY ALL MEASURES

Coming to Terms on World-Class Standards

[ALBERT SHANKER]

Many people favor establishing a national system of education standards and assessments. So do I. But are the people who are for or against such a system necessarily talking about the same things? At this point, do we know what the basic terms of the discussion even mean?

Copyright @ 1992, by Albert Shanker, former president of the American Federation of Teachers, originally published on June 17, 1992, in *Education Week,* all rights reserved, reprinted by permission.

The most basic term of all is standards. Our standards, everyone seems to agree, will be world class and the same for all students. I too believe we can and must have both excellence and equity. But what do *world-class standards* mean? I define *standards* as what we want youngsters to know and be able to do as a result of their education. Unless we're satisfied to rewrite at the national level our states' and districts' vague, motherhood-and-apple-pie education goals statements, this definition of standards inevitably must (but rarely does) bring us to the contentious issue of what students should learn and the levels of performance we should demand of them: What is good enough? What is excellent?

So when we talk about world-class standards, do we mean content standards: searching out the best international examples of what students should know and be able to do at various stages of their school career? Do we mean performance standards? If so, does that mean looking at the achievement of our competitors' best students and making their maximum our new minimum? Does it mean looking at average performances of their top, middle, and bottom or just overall averages?

I am not sure. I hear a lot about setting "standards" through a public process, which may or may not be the same thing as making our standards world-class ones. I hear a lot about developing new assessments—dangerously quick and cheap ones, technically pristine and dauntingly expensive ones—which will be pegged to world-class standards. I even hear about pilot tests based on world-class standards. But I don't hear much about examining what world-class content or performance standards are or about the relationship between the two.

If we did examine these standards, we'd find, for example, that our competitors' content standards are explicit and embodied in core curricula that all students are taught at least through elementary school. Yet mentioning a common core of learning or even national curriculum frameworks here provokes an allergic reaction. Is there justification for our optimism that we can have uniform national standards for our students without either being explicit about content or pointing to or developing some model curriculum frameworks? Can we square our rhetoric about expecting all students to meet world-class standards with the assurances being given to states, districts, and schools that they may use different curriculums to achieve those results and different assessments to measure those results? And can those different assessments given under different conditions produce results that are comparable all the way from the individual student to the national level? Some people I respect say yes, others no. Don't we need to sort out the competing answers, or at least agree on the terms used in the discussion?

If we examined world-class standards, we'd also see that they become either partially or wholly differentiated, in some places as early as fifth grade and in most places by the equivalent of our junior high or middle school. In other words, these nations track children, which we do too but dishonestly and badly. Starting around secondary school, our competitors' content and performance standards—and assessments—vary according to whether their students are aiming for an apprenticeship or for a technical school or hoping to go to a university; sometimes these standards and tests also vary by what kind of technical education or university major students intend to pursue.

I'm not saying that we should embrace these world-class practices as a model. There is a lot in them that is repugnant to our values and commitment to second, third, and more chances. The point is that there are at least three or four sets of world-class standards. The best of our competitors have much higher content and performance standards for young children than we do, and those standards, unlike ours, are uniform. The best of our competitors also have much higher content and performance standards for their university, technical college, and work-bound students than we do— and those standards are all different. None of these countries has one set of standards, world class or otherwise, that applies to all of its secondary school students, as our rhetoric is promising here.

Has our necessary preoccupation with ending different expectations for students based on group membership—race, ethnicity, class—blinded us to the fact that different students have different strengths, weaknesses, interests, and aspirations? Are we so unwilling to talk openly about differentiated standards or so paralyzed by our history of handling them inequitably that we'd rather risk massive student failure? No wonder the national standards and assessment discussion is so gun-shy about student (but not teacher) accountability! If each of our students has to meet world-class standards in each of the liberal arts and technical subjects in order to go to college or get a good job, then there will be few college students and even fewer decently paid workers. The more likely outcome of setting a single standard is a low standard, a new and higher minimum. That's movement, and that's a plus. But it's not the same thing as world-class standards. It's not the same thing as stretching everyone. And it does not get us much closer to achieving both equity and excellence.

I remain strongly committed to creating a national system of standards and assessments, and I do not expect it to be perfect at the onset. But there are lots of questions going begging, and many players using the same words and meaning different things. There's too much at stake for us not to come to terms.

Albert Shanker served as president of the American Federation of Teachers from 1974 until his death in 1997. Author of the weekly "Where We Stand" column in the *New York Times,* he was called a visionary by many. "Albert Shanker was more than just a labor leader; he was a tireless, outspoken champion of children and public schools," said Bob Chase, former president of the National Education Association.

Sacrificing democracy out of fear seems in keeping with the times. How easy it
is to forget democratic habits in times of stress, when such habits are needed most.
We are witnessing what happens to a citizenry that has not been well schooled.
I am more scared today than I was in 1992 about what is at stake in building
schools "of, for, and by the people"—democratically. When "raising test scores"
becomes the only definition we offer the young of what we admire and value—
of what it is to achieve—we have lost our way.—DM

PUBLISHED JUNE 17, 1992

BY ALL
MEASURES

"Just Another False Chase"

[DEBORAH MEIER]

The pressure to look for answers via national curriculum and national testing is wrongheaded, dangerous, and counterproductive. At best it's a waste of
resources; at worst it will injure American democracy. Most likely it will be
just another false chase.

We are on the brink of an important and hopefully exciting new age for
education. The American public school system did what was asked of it a
century ago. The new century demands a very different kind of institution.
The change is as dramatic as the transformation of a horse-and-buggy society into an automotive society. What is required will be a change in the way
people think.

To try to mandate and regulate what schools should teach and how to teach it is wrongheaded. Testing is a powerful way to maintain practice, but a terrible way to unleash the kind of entrepreneurial risk taking, the kind of intelligent practice, that is desperately needed by tomorrow's professionals.

We tried to change mathematics education this way a generation ago. The ideas were right. The mathematics profession today has not come up with better ones. It is simply trying once again to find a way to influence its practitioners to adopt a more thoughtful and contemporary mathematical pedagogy. Last time the strategy was top-down. It influenced testing, text-book publishers, and curriculum designers. But neither teachers nor parents understood the changes; they conformed outwardly and balked inwardly. The reforms became the stuff of jokes, and our kids were shortchanged.

Similarly, when I entered education in the 1960s, I was told that my "slow" and steady ideas for reform were not responsive enough to the crisis in literacy. We needed to get Johnny reading in a hurry. So, against the advice of those who knew schools best, we stepped up the pressure via de-mands for improved test scores. We decided to hold teachers, schools, and kids accountable for results. We got the results. Higher test scores came pouring in, but not better-educated and more-literate students. New York City's scores went from nearly two-thirds reading below "national norms" to less than one-half in 10 years. Miracle of miracles. And the new scores have held and improved steadily ever since. But what about reading? No one I know claims our students are reading more or reading better. They tell us this time they'll have better instruments. But even the leading expert psy-chometrician of them all, the Educational Testing Service's Greg Anrig, is dubious of that claim.

Whether we can or should ever devise a single central system for moni-toring real intellectual achievement, I do not know. I am among the doubters. I think a democratic society requires a continual debate about the meaning of being well educated. Testing stifles such debate. I think the quality about America that all the world loves is precisely our irreverence: a willingness to challenge authority, to question those in the know. How to preserve that irreverence while also fostering greater respect for intellectual achieve-ment should not be decided quickly or thoughtlessly, under the pressure for quickie test results. More centralizing, more "thought control," is unwise and unwarranted.

And as a school person, I know also that it is counterproductive. We are just beginning to see the fruits of the new ideas that emerged in the '80s— the ideas represented by such leaders as Ted Sizer, John Goodlad, Howard Gardner, James Comer, and so on. We are on the verge of seeing new approaches to assessment flourish, as different schools and systems try different methods. And quite likely what we will discover is that no one approach will do the job, but all are useful for different folks at different times in the process of reform. Federal assistance directed at supporting these varied efforts to get the incentives right, on the one hand, and the information needed right, on the other hand, can be very useful. Funds for on-site research are desperately needed. Retooling schooling requires research and development.

Meanwhile, the National Assessment of Educational Progress, if continued on a sampled basis, can keep us abreast of what's happening, to provide an honest, if limited, thermometer. Anything more intrusive will kill the baby. The baby is just waking up from a long sleep; nurture her, don't kill her in a new bureaucratic testing and measuring morass.

Deborah Meier has spent four decades working in and writing about public schools. She is founder of a network of small public elementary and secondary schools in New York City and Boston, including the Central Park East schools in East Harlem. Currently she is a senior scholar and adjunct professor at New York University's Steinhardt School of Education.

For the past seven years I have been embedded in a major school system that has been generating results that external foundation and university observers frequently classify as miracles. While the researchers have been trying to understand the "whats" that have apparently been so effective, I have been documenting the "hows." What has emerged is a supportive scaffold for *all* the district's work, from classroom to boardroom. This enables the district to drive standards-based reforms from the inside out. The district now has a standard practice for collaboratively solving the daily problems of learning and teaching. That is the only place the journey to No Child Left Behind's future can start.—LAR

PUBLISHED APRIL 6, 1993

IS THERE A STANDARD FOR MEETING STANDARDS?

[LEWIS A. RHODES]

Over the past several years we have focused on the setting and assessing of standards for K-12 education, paying scant attention to the warnings of local practitioners. These practitioners have cautioned that separate standards-development efforts could create a smorgasbord of incompatible criteria for whose attainment they will be held accountable. They also point out that although assessing success and ensuring success are related processes, present "outside-in" efforts have it backwards. Supposedly parallel assessment processes are being developed as an overlay on the work of schools and classrooms, not as an integral function aimed at increasing daily effectiveness.

In effect, current standards-setting and assessment-development processes are defining the beginning and end points of a journey that America's schools are expected to undertake. At one end, assessments documenting the current status of American schools—such as those of the National Education Goals Panel—are beginning to provide a snapshot of the starting point. At the same time, the various groups defining world-class standards for how America's students must perform are picturing where schools must go. In the gap between that beginning and end, one finds little coherent, coordinated national effort to suggest and support the best ways of getting there—that is, standards for meeting the standards. (The opportunity-to-learn standards and strategies envisioned in the new Goals 2000: Educate America Act will primarily address resource requirements, not how to apply them to attain desired ends.)

In the local world of public education, meanwhile, the processes for meeting new (or for that matter, old) standards have become a hodgepodge of multiple theories and strategies for curriculum content and organization, instruction, and school structure. But there is yet no clear agreement on the real task: how to address the interdependence of each of those areas so that entire organizations move on a continuing journey of incremental change as part of their daily work.

The negative consequences of this missing standard can be seen in major school districts. In one well-publicized urban district, 26 national foundations or reform groups have developed collaborative initiatives and partnerships. Somewhere in this district's schools one can find an example of every major school reform being considered today, including the state's new curriculum frameworks. Yet with no regular way for the district to learn from these pilot settings what it needs to know to address the needs of all its students, the 26 well-intentioned change efforts actually suboptimize the district's capabilities to transform itself.

ARE THERE STANDARDS FOR MEETING STANDARDS? Any organization whose work integrates diverse efforts to attain common purposes or results employs a fundamental—if not implicit—process standard that influences the nature of continuing choices and decisions at all levels. In the physical world of travel, this process is called navigation; in the psychological world it is called trial-and-error learning. Both purpose-driven processes are characterized by a fundamental principle: Regardless of where you are going, you have to start from where you are. From that point on, the process continually feeds the creation of understanding how to get there.

In the management world of human service organizations (other than education), the starting point for standards-driven daily work is the current status of the individual before them. Core organizational processes are aligned to support the continuing diagnostic-prescriptive decisions of first-line practitioners.

Even nonservice industries have belatedly recognized that their responses too must start with the present needs or requirements of their "customer." In fact, a world-class process standard—a standard for meeting standards—is emerging. The common structural core of world-class organizations—regardless of the nature of their services or products—is a systematic process that allows improvement to be a continuing and supported part of the entire organization's daily work. This process may be called Continuous Quality Improvement (CQI), Total Quality Management (TQM), or sometimes even just quality. Whatever the label, quality management's systemically applied systematic strategies and tools provide ways to structure the interactions necessary for the organization to learn from its work. Organizational transformation becomes the consequence of that learning.

One way to envision how this plays out is to picture the structure on a traditional organizational chart. Leaders in successful world-class work settings create a connected learning infrastructure that fills in the spaces between the boxes. They link the people whose daily decisions and choices move the organization toward its goals, purposes, or standards.

In other words, quality management formalizes the informal structure of an organization—the problem-driven interactions and information exchange usually left to chance meetings, grapevines, and other informal, individual get-togethers. As such, it is standard driven, content free, and manageable. Leaders can be held accountable for its results.

{ **BUT WHAT ABOUT SCHOOLS?** The logical question for those concerned with systemic transformation of K-12 education through standards and assessments is to what extent that task can be addressed through the types of world-class process standards that are associated with quality management. In the past several years, educators have not been far behind their private-sector counterparts in sensing that the theories, strategies, and tools of quality management have some relevance to their work—and have similarly been struggling to figure out how it fits with what they know they have to do.

But the current national debate on opportunity-to-learn standards suggests that there exists a fundamental barrier to the acceptance of these process standards for the daily work of schools. Local school practitioners—who will be accountable for meeting new national and state standards—are handicapped by two "naive" theories about the work that takes place in schools (that is, theories developed from direct observation such as, the Earth is flat, the sun and planets circle the Earth, or heavy objects fall faster than lighter ones just because they appear to). One such unquestioned theory deals with the observed work of schools as a delivery process, the other with the role of the teacher as an isolated practitioner performing repetitive tasks who does not need or have time to learn from her or his work.

The delivery paradigm frames the actions of some curriculum reformers who believe that schools "transmit," "communicate," or "transfer" knowledge. Yet practitioners who work in schools every day know that they no more deliver instruction than hospitals deliver medicine. Modern hospitals, however, do deliver appropriate medicine because they are structured around an information-driven process standard that allows continuing generation and analysis of individual assessment information. This supports diagnostic decisions about appropriate medicine and other interventions that meet the requirements of world-class wellness standards.

The isolated-professional paradigm shapes many actions of those who think teacher autonomy is the answer to better schools. They assume that local school practitioners already know how to function in new roles and relationships, and need only to be freed to act. Returning to the hospital analogy, medical professionals have autonomy—interdependent autonomy. They recognize that autonomy without knowledge and collaborative support is not freedom.

As local educators have begun to explore the meaning of CQI. or TQM., they are discovering a base of knowledge about schools as connected systems of intrinsically driven knowledge workers that shatters these old theories much as Copernicus's understanding destroyed the Ptolemaic paradigm.

What is emerging from their work with quality management in schooling is a systemic view of a school district as a managed supportive infrastructure—one that provides the technical, social, and psychological context to support the fundamental trial-and-error nature of individual decisions that strive to respond to human needs.

This infrastructure of work roles and relationships provides:

- Regular opportunities for reflection, learning, and planning as part of daily work

- Regular access to hard data on results and soft data in the form of shared expertise and experiences

- Tools and processes to focus everyone's knowledge and effort on the core functions of teaching and learning

- Support for the development of new, more effective, and satisfying roles for all staff members

WHAT WILL IT TAKE? If the current national standards debate is an example, these local learnings about process standards and accountability are not effectively trickling up. Yet understanding the need for and feasibility of these ideas cannot wait for research to "prove" their effectiveness. If schools are to have the support required to meet world-class standards, we must make visible this universal management process standard. Policymakers must become aware of the power of this type of process—one that systemically supports and enables its participants to learn how to improve and institutionalize improvements as part of the job. Federal and state policies must support local development of an accountable process infrastructure—framed by learning standards and fed by continuing assessment information—that aligns all roles and relationships to the core functions of teaching and learning.

Without such a manageable, widely applicable process standard, the only thing bridging the gap between where schools are and where they must be will be the hides of local practitioners, who once more will be blamed for not already knowing how to get there.

Organizational transformation, management expert W. Edwards Deming noted, is a "journey." To attempt that crossing without standard tools for navigating through dynamically changing conditions would not be tolerated in any modern endeavor—except schools.

Lewis A. Rhodes was associate executive director of the American Association of School Administrators when he wrote this essay. Today he continues as a thinking partner with leaders and others most concerned with creating, from the inside out, sustainable systemic changes in the policies and practices of school systems, and developing leaders who can do it.

While educational practices change slowly, educational debates may
swiftly become anachronistic. A scant dozen years after this Commentary was
published, there is little public debate about disciplinary standards; virtually no one
remembers the National Education Standards and Improvement Council—the
body charged with accrediting standards. Standard setting occurs at the state level,
the least controversial standards are embraced, and far more effort is spent "teaching
to the state test" than in developing robust skills and understandings. Texas improves,
but only by Texan standards. I am less sanguine about the possibility of meaningful
standards in our disunited States. I quote Winston Churchill: "The American people
always do the right thing, but only after they've tried every other alternative."—HG

PUBLISHED SEPTEMBER 7, 1994

THE NEED FOR ANTI-BABEL STANDARDS

[HOWARD GARDNER]

About the last thing we need these days is a new variety of standards in
the education reform movement. Talk of standards began but a decade ago.
Soon the descriptors *national* and *voluntary* were added. Then an important
distinction was introduced between *content* standards, which stipulate the
kinds of knowledge and skills students should master, and *performance*
standards, which indicate the actual level of performance a student must
achieve if he or she is to be credited with meeting a given standard.

The Goals 2000 legislation introduced yet another significant kind—*delivery* or *opportunity-to-learn* standards. Suppose the content standard holds that a student should be able to write an effective letter to the editor, and a performance standard indicates which specimen letter qualifies as effective and which does not. Let's say that a student proves unable to write such a letter. Should the student be penalized, even barred from graduation? Only, says the legislation, if that student has had a genuine opportunity to learn, as measured by such indices as qualified teachers, adequate offerings, readily available resources and technologies, a safe environment, reasonable assessments, and other features "the council deems appropriate." And indeed we have a new federally appointed body, the National Education Standards and Improvement Council, or NESIC, whose assignment it is to examine various proposed standards and certify those judged to be adequate.

On any analysis, the national standards council faces a formidable challenge. Following the admirable example of the National Council of Teachers of Mathematics, nearly every professional disciplinary association either has or will shortly finish preparing its list of standards. Many states, and other jurisdictions and agencies as well, will shortly have their standards drafted. If the documents prepared so far are any indication, descriptions of content, performance, and delivery standards will take up hundreds of pages and will feature dozens, if not hundreds, of separate requirements. (It is always easier to add than to pare.) One can readily envision a scenario where NESIC—with its small budget and slender staff—will have to judge dozens of sets of standards and do so in a way that can withstand not only the scrutiny of critical educators but also challenges in the courts. For if any set of certified standards becomes used for consequences (and if they are not so used, they are destined to be ignored), any group that feels the standards are unfair will have the right to mount a legal challenge.

One can imagine the cartoons now, one can anticipate the skits on *Saturday Night Live,* or the spoofs from the ever-eager lips of Rush Limbaugh. Hapless teachers, students, and parents are burdened with numerous sets of standards, some very grand, some very detailed, some progressive, some traditional. The effort it will take simply to assimilate the standards will be enormous; then to implement them, to assess them, to relate them to ultimate employment opportunities, to defend them in court—well, the mind boggles.

So why should anyone even dare to think of a new kind of standard? Precisely because of the Babel or pandemonium that is likely to result if the relations that obtain among certified standards are not themselves carefully weighed. If, as appears likely (if not legally mandated), NESIC certifies standards on their own merits, one is likely to face a situation where the standards from disparate domains bear little relationship to one another, or even contradict one another. A veritable welter of incommensurate standards is readily predictable. And so, with tongue only barely in cheek, I insist here on the need for Anti-Babel (or as a secular variant, Anti-Babble) standards.

If we are to have national or state standards that fit together, that complement rather than contradict one another, the certifying body needs to take into account three separate facets:

1. *Fit among bodies of knowledge.* Over the centuries, different disciplines, subdisciplines, and interdisciplinary specialties have arisen. Some may fit together comfortably, but others may abrade or even contradict one another. We cannot afford to propound, within a jurisdiction, one approach to history—say, an approach that focuses on themes; a second approach to science—say, one that focuses on problem solving; a third approach to mathematics—say, one that focuses on problem finding or memorization of facts or creation of new mathematical systems. Like it or not, the standards council must be prepared to don an epistemological hat.

2. *Fit for teachers.* When teachers are in charge of the entire curriculum, as is typically the case in the early grades, the various sets of standards need to fit together comfortably for the preparation of classes and the teaching and evaluation of students. And when students are working with several teachers during the day, it is perhaps even more important that the messages and methods of these teachers be consistent with one another.

3. *Fit for students.* In the end, we want students to develop a single, powerful mind, housing strands of knowledge that can be integrated and synthesized. This is no easy accomplishment, even when a single teacher has created the curriculum. We can anticipate enormous confusion on the part of students if the various certified curricula have not been fashioned with a sensitivity to how students relate ideas, themes, practices to one another. Student schizophrenia is as likely as teacher or epistemological schizophrenia.

Are there any elements in current school reform that are attending to such a need for fit, that are devising inoculations against the Babel peril? Current efforts at producing integrated pedagogies for the middle grades, or curricula organized around "essential questions" or "generative ideas" in high school, seek fits that make sense for students and teachers. It must be noted, however, that proponents of these innovative approaches tend to be very suspicious of the national standards movement. Indeed, critics like Theodore Sizer, Linda Darling-Hammond, and Deborah Meier see the current standards movements, organized largely around the traditional disciplines, as being inimical to their own preferred views of school reform.

We must face the possibility that the national standards movement, motivated by the best of intentions, may fall apart, like a crumbling Babel; or that it may end up by crippling some of the most promising reform efforts under way in our country.

To forestall these possibilities, I offer three suggestions to NESIC and to NESIC watchers, within and outside of government:

1. Encourage submission of standards by bodies that are not restricted to traditional disciplinary boundaries. Develop criteria for judging such school-based initiatives. Be prepared to offer certification to the curriculum of New York City's Central Park East Secondary School, for example.

2. Insist that submissions by more traditional groups address the Babel problem. Unless a submitter can demonstrate that its content standards can fit comfortably with those submitted by other disciplines or groups, send the submitter back to the standards drawing board.

3. Deemphasize certification and focus energies instead on the development of standards that will facilitate better teaching and learning. The national educational standards board might actually turn out to be more benevolent, and perhaps even more powerful, if it ceded (or at least downplayed) its certification prerogatives; it could instead provide detailed feedback on the strengths and weaknesses of submissions, coupled with strong suggestions about how proposed standards might work effectively in different kinds of schools featuring different kinds of curricula.

Before assuming that the power to certify is what confers legitimacy, recall that some of the most important voices in the country—for example, reports offered by the National Academy of Sciences—are advisory only. And recall as well that states have, in effect, been certifying standards for decades, without increased performance resulting. What we need in the country, as a means of improving education, is not more certifying bodies. We need parents and communities who are involved, teachers who are professional enough to devise and critique standards, students who want to use their minds well. A reconceived NESIC could catalyze more sophisticated discussion; it could showcase examples of how to bring about more effective educational practices and how to stimulate students to learn well and to want to learn more.

Howard Gardner is Hobbs Professor of Cognition and Education at the Harvard Graduate School of Education. He is also author of more than 20 books, including *The Disciplined Mind: Beyond Facts and Standardized Tests, The K-12 Education That Every Child Deserves* (Penguin Putnam, 2000), and *Intelligence Reframed* (Basic Books, 2000).

My embarrassment over devoting an entire Commentary to so simple a thesis—
that increased difficulty is not tantamount to higher quality—is exceeded by my
distress that this fact has eluded so many people. I wrote this essay before the crude
push to "raise standards" was nationalized, before yet another effort to reform
secondary education turned out to mean just making it harder. Several states have
worried that too many students are doing well on their tests and have raised the
passing grade. High schools are actually ranked on the basis of how many Advanced
Placement courses they offer, even though such courses often merely accelerate the
worst sort of traditional instruction. Nothing would please me more than to learn that
my essay was no longer relevant; sadly, nothing could be further from the truth.—AK

PUBLISHED SEPTEMBER 15, 1999

CONFUSING HARDER WITH BETTER

[ALFIE KOHN]

Never underestimate the power of a catchy slogan and a false dichotomy.
When a politician pronounces himself a supporter of "law and order" or
"a strong defense," you may protest that it's not that simple, but even as
you start to explain why, you've already been dismissed as soft on crime or
unwilling to defend Our Way of Life.

People who attend to nuance have long been at a disadvantage in politics,
where spin is out of control. Never before, however, has the same been quite

so true of the public conversation about education, which is distinguished today by simplistic demands for "accountability" and "raising the bar." Not only public officials but business groups and many journalists as well have played a role in reducing the available options to two: either you are in favor of higher standards or you are presumably content with lower standards. Choose one.

These days almost anything, no matter how ill-considered, can be done to students and to schools, as long as it is done in the name of raising standards. As a result, we are facing a situation in this country that can be described without exaggeration as an educational emergency: the intellectual life is being squeezed out of classrooms, schools are being turned into giant test-prep centers, and many students—as well as some of our finest educators—are being forced out.

Part of the problem is that the enterprise of raising standards in practice means little more than raising the scores on standardized tests, many of which are norm-referenced, multiple-choice, and otherwise flawed. The more schools commit themselves to improving performance on these tests, the more meaningful opportunities to learn are sacrificed. Thus high scores are often a sign of *lowered* standards—a paradox rarely appreciated by those who make, or report on, education policy.

Compounding the problem is a reliance on the sort of instruction that treats children as passive receptacles into which knowledge or skills are poured. "Back to basics" education—a misnomer, really, because most American schools never left it—might be described as outdated except for the fact that there never was a time when it worked all that well. Modern cognitive science just explains more systematically why this approach has always come up short. When you watch students slogging through textbooks, memorizing lists, being lectured at, and working on isolated skills, you begin to realize that nothing bears a greater responsibility for undermining educational excellence than the continued dominance of traditional instruction. Shrill calls for "accountability" usually just produce an accelerated version of the same thing.

Underlying the kind of pedagogy and assessment associated with the tougher-standards movement is an assumption that has rarely been identified and analyzed—namely, that the main thing wrong with the schools today is that kids get off too easy. Texts and tests and teaching have been "dumbed down," it is alleged. At the heart of metaphors like *raising* standards (or the bar) is the premise that harder is better.

Now, the first and most obvious thing to be said in response is that assignments and exams can be too difficult just as they can be too easy. If the latter can leave students insufficiently challenged, the former can make them feel stupid, which in turn can lead them to feel alienated, to lose interest in the subject matter, and sometimes to misbehave. (It's usually less threatening for kids to be seen as incorrigible than as inadequate.) Anyone can ask students questions that are laughably easy *or* impossibly difficult. "The trick," observed Jerome Bruner, "is to find the medium questions that can be answered and that take you somewhere." In short, maximum difficulty isn't the same as optimal difficulty.

But let's delve a little deeper. Maybe the issue isn't whether harder is always better so much as why we focus so much attention on the whole question of difficulty.

John Dewey reminded us that the value of what students do "resides in its connection with a stimulation of greater *thoughtfulness,* not in the greater strain it imposes." If you were making a list of what counts in education—that is, the criteria to use in judging whether students would benefit from what they were doing—the task's difficulty level would be only one factor among many, and almost certainly not the most important. To judge schools by how demanding they are is rather like judging an opera on the basis of how many notes it contains that are hard for singers to hit. In other words, it leaves out most of what matters.

Here's what follows from this recognition: if homework assignments or exams consist of factual-recall questions, it really doesn't make all that much difference whether there are 25 tough questions or 10 easy ones. Similarly, a textbook does not become a more appropriate teaching tool just because it is intended for a higher grade level. Some parents indignantly complain that their kids are bored and can complete the worksheets without breaking a sweat. They ought to be complaining about the fact that the teacher is relying on worksheets at all. Likewise, some teachers disdain any colleague who spoon-feeds information, insisting (often with a tone of self-congratulation) that in *their* classrooms, students have to *work*! But the latter may not be any better than the former, and the two together constitute a false dichotomy.

We have to look at the whole method of instruction, the underlying theory of learning, rather than just quibble about how hard the assignment is or how much the students must strain.

One reason a back-to-basics curriculum fits perfectly with the philosophy of prizing hard work is that it *creates* hard work—often unnecessarily. It's more difficult to learn to read if the task is to decode a string of phonemes than if it is to make sense of interesting stories. It's more exhausting to memorize a list of scientific vocabulary words than it is to learn scientific concepts by devising your own experiment. If kids are going to be forced to learn facts without context and skills without meaning, it's certainly handy to have an ideology that values difficulty for its own sake. To be sure, learning often requires sustained attention and effort. But there's a vital difference between that which is rigorous and that which is merely onerous.

Other words are similarly slippery. Do we want students to be *challenged* more, or to live up to *higher expectations* in a school that stands for *excellence*? It all depends on how these words are being defined. If they signify a deeper, richer, more engaging curriculum in which students play an active role in integrating ideas and pursuing controversial questions, then you can count on my support. But if these terms are used to justify memorizing more state capitals, or getting a student to bring up her grades (a process that research has shown often undermines the quality of learning), then it's not so clear that rigor and challenge and all the rest of it are worth supporting.

If these distinctions are missed by some parents and teachers, they are systematically ignored by the purveyors of tougher standards. Recently my own state introduced a test that students will soon have to pass in order to receive a high school diploma. It requires them to acquire a staggering number of facts, which allowed policymakers to claim proudly that they had raised the bar. After new proficiency exams were failed by a significant proportion of students in several other states, education officials there responded by making the tests even harder the following year. The commissioner of education for Colorado offered some insight into the sensibility underlying such decisions: "Unless you get bad results," he declared, "it is highly doubtful you have done anything useful with your tests. Low scores have become synonymous with good tests." Such is the logic on which the tougher-standards movement has been built.

But how many adults could pass these exams? How many high school teachers possess the requisite stock of information outside their own subjects? How many college professors, for that matter, or business executives, or state legislators could confidently write an essay about Mayan agricultural practices or divergent plate boundaries?

We would do well to adopt (Deborah) Meier's Mandate: *No student should be expected to meet an academic requirement that a cross section of successful adults in the community cannot.*

(In the same spirit, I propose Kohn's Corollary to Meier's Mandate: All persons given to pious rhetoric about the need to "raise standards" and produce "world-class academic performance for the 21st century" not only should be required to take these exams themselves but must agree to have their scores published in the newspaper.)

Beyond the issue of how many of us could meet these standards is an equally provocative question: How many of us *need* to know this stuff—not just on the basis of job requirements but as a reflection of what it means to be well-educated? Do these facts and skills reflect what we honor, what matters to us about schooling and human life? Often the standards being rammed into our children's classrooms are not merely unreasonable but irrelevant. It is the kinds of things students are being forced to learn, and the approach to learning itself, that don't ring true. The tests that result—for students and sometimes for teachers—are not just ridiculously difficult but simply ridiculous.

"It is not enough to be busy," Henry David Thoreau once remarked. "The question is, what are we busy about?" If our students are memorizing more forgettable facts than ever before, if they are spending their hours being drilled on what will help them ace a standardized test, then we may indeed have raised the bar—and more's the pity. In that case, school may be harder, but it sure as hell isn't any better.

Alfie Kohn is author of 11 books about education and human behavior, including *The Schools Our Children Deserve: Moving Beyond Traditional Classrooms and "Tougher Standards"* (Mariner Books, 2000); *What Does It Mean to Be Well Educated? And Other Essays on Standards, Grading, and Other Follies* (Beacon Press, 2004); and *The Homework Myth* (Da Capo Lifelong Books, 2006). He lives (actually) in the Boston area and (virtually) at www.alfiekohn.org.

"In contradiction to the theory of social determinism, breadth of knowledge is a far greater factor in achievement than socioeconomic status. . . . This little-known and quite momentous fact means that imparting broad knowledge to all children is the single most effective way to narrow the competence gap between demographic groups through schooling. The tests we give should reflect our understanding of this truth."—Excerpted from *The Knowledge Deficit* by E. D. Hirsch Jr.*

PUBLISHED FEBRUARY 2, 2000

THE TESTS WE NEED

[E. D. HIRSCH JR.]

Statewide content standards are beginning to spawn high-stakes tests that have evoked furious opposition—not without cause. The greatest outcry (to reach my ears) has been occurring in Virginia and Massachusetts, where the new tests are based on fairly specific content standards. In Kentucky and Maryland, where the high-stakes tests are based on vague general skills more than on specific curriculum content, the protests seem mild by contrast. Yet despite the louder outcry against curriculum-based tests, I believe they hold far more promise than skills-based tests to promote significant gains in achievement and equity.

*At the author's request, the editors used a brief excerpt from his book *The Knowledge Deficit* (Houghton Mifflin, 2006) for his Commentary update.

It has to be conceded that, under present circumstances, the backlash against curriculum-based tests has been warranted. The policymakers who have instituted these high-stakes tests have made two strategic mistakes. First, they have introduced content standards and tests before providing teachers and students with detailed outlines and teaching materials that define what the content standards really are. They have put in place no adequate system for training teachers in the subject matters identified by the content standards. They have failed to do the hard work of deciding which aspects of the content are the most essential to be included in textbooks, teacher seminars, and tests—a lack of specificity and selectivity that has made at least some of the tests less reasonable and fair than they should be.

Between the furious opponents of the curriculum-based tests and their determined advocates there seems to be no middle ground. Yet each party seems right in some respects—except for the antitest extremists who want no objective statewide tests at all. The more reasonable critics of curriculum-based tests rightly object to inadequate guidelines and materials, and occasional flaws in the tests themselves, and they correctly observe that five decades of content-indifferent schooling and content-poor teacher preparation cannot be reversed overnight.

On the other side, determined test advocates are right that curriculum-based tests are the fairest and most effective means of achieving the aims of democratic schooling. Test advocates should accept the reality that the needed improvements in teacher preparation, in teaching materials, and in the tests themselves cannot occur overnight. But I find myself squarely on the side of the test advocates in resisting any attempt to exploit the necessary slowness of the process as an excuse simply to call a moratorium on curriculum standards and curriculum-based tests. They are the most promising educational development in half a century.

How these curriculum-based tests should be phased in as criteria for student promotion and graduation is a practical and political question to be decided in a democracy by the representatives of the people. I want to shed light on a technical issue that can be useful in helping to make such policy decisions better informed—that is the differences and the connections between competency-based tests and curriculum-based tests.

Competency-based tests sample knowledge from a very broad range of domains, which enables the tests to exhibit a reliably high correlation between test scores and real-world competencies. Curriculum-based tests are narrower. They try to determine how well specific content standards in a particular domain for a particular age group have been learned. Whereas competency tests indicate overall achieved ability, curriculum tests indicate whether specific knowledge has been gained. The astute reader will perhaps see where I am going—that a well-devised curriculum, monitored by good curriculum-based tests should, over time, extend the breadth of a student's knowledge and thus raise scores on broad-gauged competency-based tests.

Since an indispensable aim of schooling is to increase student competency, the public has a right to demand that results on the two kinds of test should in due course show a positive correlation. A main purpose of this essay is to explain why good curriculum-based tests, based on good content standards, are the surest and most democratic means of raising scores on competency-based tests and achieving real-world competencies.

An excellent example of competency-based tests would be standardized reading tests, such as the verbal portions of the Stanford Achievement Test-Ninth Edition, the Iowa Tests of Basic Skills, the Nelson-Denny Reading Test, and so on. While these are norm-referenced instruments, which rank students against each other in percentiles, they can also be scored to indicate a student's grade level of reading comprehension. A score of 5.2 would mean that the student is reading at the level the average student has reached by the second month of grade 5. These grade-level calibrations (which have been criticized on various grounds) could also be translated into absolute scores, which can be equated over many decades. All of the well-established reading tests are valid, reliable, and highly correlated with one another.

What sorts of questions are asked on a standardized reading test that cause it to indicate academic achievement and readiness so reliably? In the earliest-grade versions, there are of course questions about sounds and letters. Later versions include questions about vocabulary, the meanings of individual sentences, and the implications of passages from literature, the natural sciences, the social sciences, practical affairs, and several other domains.

How could such a test, disconnected from any specific curriculum, so reliably calibrate academic achievement, learning readiness, and even real-world competency? One needs not just to offer the ample evidence that this claim is true, but also to provide a credible theory that explains the strong correlation between reading and general competency.

To the extent that any clear theory at all underlies much educational research, it is often unspoken and may be inconsistent with widely accepted scientific opinion. In the sciences, a damaging criticism in peer review is to call a research finding *a-theoretical*. Ever since Pierre Duhem (*The Aim and Structure of Physical Theory,* 1905), such indifference to theory has been understood as a scientific weakness, because empirical evidence can always be interpreted in multiple ways.

For instance, the claim that the planets go in complicated orbits round the Earth rather than the sun fits the observational facts; it's just not a highly probable theory.

The problem of a-theoreticity is especially severe in educational research, which is beset by a blizzard of uncontrolled variables, such as teacher quality and outside-school influences, whose effects cannot be estimated confidently without applying the most plausible theory.

So I think it will be useful to state some of the theoretical principles that explain why good competency tests in reading turn out to be powerfully indicative of achieved abilities that go far beyond reading. Such a theory has the additional benefit of explaining the potency of curriculum-based tests.

1. *Reading has been shown to be a process of mentally rephonicizing language, rather than being a separate linguistic process.* The interpretation of the written word is a reenactment of the interpretation of the spoken word. Many of the conventions used in written language are used in speaking and listening. This mental reenactment of speech explains why reading ability is correlated with general communicative competence—the ability to understand and make oneself understood in oral as well as written speech.

2. *Such general communicative competence is required for effective social intercourse in modern society* and is especially critical in schooling, where it forms the basis for understanding the oral and written communications of other people, including teachers.

3. *The level of one's reading ability (as reflected in the vocabulary items and passage types on a reading test) predicts the level of one's ability to learn new things.* A person learns new things by associating them with things already known. Scoring high on a reading test requires a broad vocabulary, which represents broad knowledge that offers multiple points of association for gaining further knowledge. The more you know, the easier it is to learn still more—a principle well-established in cognitive psychology.

This is the critical element of the theory. Breadth of knowledge is the single factor within human control that contributes most to academic achievement and general cognitive competence. Breadth of knowledge is a far greater factor, for instance, than socioeconomic status. The positive correlation between achieved ability and socioeconomic status is .422, whereas the correlation between achieved ability and general information is .811. This little-known and quite momentous fact means that imparting broad knowledge to all children is the single most effective means of narrowing the competence gap through schooling.

4. *A score on a test of reading ability shows the degree to which this broad knowledge is readily deployable.* A merely passive vocabulary that cannot be marshaled and used critically for reading comprehension is inert knowledge. Psychologists use terms like *accessibility* and *availability* to describe such actively usable knowledge. Accessibility of knowledge is attested to by a person's ability to bring that knowledge to bear in comprehending and analyzing the diverse passages in the test.

In sum, theory predicts that a good reading test will indicate students' level of communicative competence, their breadth of knowledge, and their ability to apply that knowledge to learning new things. Theory further predicts that these competencies will correlate well with job performance and the capacity to be an active citizen, because communicative competence and the ability to learn new things are highly important skills in meeting the duties and responsibilities of the modern world.

These predictions are confirmed by massive evidence.

Scores on early reading tests predict scores on later reading tests. The more one reads, the more automated becomes the process, and through reading itself the broader becomes one's knowledge and vocabulary, and consequently the more readily one understands ever more difficult matter.

Scores on reading tests predict grades in school. There is a positive correlation between reading scores and academic achievement.

Scores on reading tests predict job performance. Obviously, reading scores do not predict whether somebody can fix your car's engine. But according to studies conducted by the armed services, reading scores do predict how readily and well a person will learn to fix your car's engine.

Scores on reading tests predict income. Given the causal connections between communicative ability, learning ability, and job performance, it is not surprising that superior job skill should be rewarded, on average, with superior pay.

The scores on a reading test or other competency test may sometimes be relatively independent of the quality of schooling. One's reading score is better predicted by one's family environment and the amount of reading one has done than by the school one attends.

This is a version of the finding by James S. Coleman that influences outside the school are more determinative of academic achievement than influences inside the school. This is not an inevitable sociological law but rather a persistent feature of current American schooling, and it does not hold with the same force in France or Sweden. The gap-closing educational results in these countries remind us that an important purpose of democratic schooling is to help able people overcome accidents of birth and circumstance. I believe that educational policy in a democracy should aim to create a system of schooling in which scores on reading tests depend much more on school influences than they recently have in the United States.

Schools can accomplish this egalitarian purpose by making students better readers, that is, by causing them to score higher on competency tests, whether or not they come from educated homes. This goal can be reached only by an effective, cumulative curriculum that gradually builds up the knowledge and vocabulary that are being sampled in a reading test. This seems to me a criterion that should be met by state curriculum standards: Will teaching this content provide children with high communicative competence and the ability to learn new things, no matter what their home disadvantages may be?

This democratic criterion means putting in place the very policies that have created the current backlash—setting forth grade-by-grade knowledge standards and monitoring whether that knowledge is being gained, an aim that has won strong support in low-income districts, which recognize the democratic effect of this reform.

John Bishop of Cornell University has shown that educational systems that require definite content standards and that use curriculum-based tests to determine whether the curriculum has been learned greatly improve achievement for all students, including those from less advantaged backgrounds. Additional evidence in support of curriculum-based testing comes from the recent finding that gains in reading are directly proportional to the completeness with which a school implements a coherent, content-rich curriculum.

Put starkly, a system of coherent standards coupled with curriculum-based tests will in fact cause achievement on *non*-curriculum-based tests to rise. It will result in higher achievement overall and a narrowing of the academic gap between rich and poor.

But this change must be instituted wisely, and the critical policy decisions must not be left to technical test-makers. Testing companies are very good at creating instruments that have good "psychometric properties," that is, that rank-order students in a smooth, normal curve.

Curriculum-based tests should not exhibit those statistical properties, at least not at first. The tests should mainly discriminate between the students who have gained essential knowledge and those who haven't, with maybe one further category for students who give an abundance of right answers. The earliest versions of the new tests shouldn't rank-order students beyond those three categories—fail, pass, superior. Later on, in a mature, content-based system, such as those Bishop studied, more refined scores might be appropriate.

To grasp the distinction between fancy test items, which aren't appropriate, and plain ones, which are, consider the following examples:

The Civil War ended in: (a) 1864 (b) 1865 (c) 1866 (d) 1867.

The Civil War ended in: (a) 1812 (b) 1830 (c) 1865 (d) 1880.

Few will doubt that the first question will do a better job of inducing incorrect answers. By including plenty of hard items, test-makers can ensure refined, neat rank orderings among students. But it should not be left up to test-makers, or even to ad hoc advisory committees, to decide whether students at a particular grade level should have such exactitude of knowledge. That decision should be made and announced in advance by those officials who create the standards and the supporting materials. Curriculum-based exams best serve their purpose, at least at first, by being straightforward and unpedantic.

These considerations lead me to suggest that state education officials should do the following:

- Recognize that we are in a transition period, after half a century of content-meager schooling, and that state departments of education must provide the means for teaching and learning the required content standards before too much weight is placed on them. Low stakes before high stakes. Given the historical context, that's only fair.

- Make public in a very clear and detailed fashion the important aspects of the content standards that are to be emphasized in teacher training, textbooks, and curriculum-based tests.

- Use the tests as devices to focus effort on productive and important learning that yields centrally useful knowledge and high competence.

- Grade the straightforward tests generously on a pass-fail basis (with perhaps a "superior" for answering a very high number of straightforward questions) during the transition period while teachers are being trained and appropriate textbooks are being created.

- Offer, apart from the official, secure tests, informal, no-stakes, year-by-year diagnostic tests, which will enable schools to detect knowledge deficits and monitor student progress.

- Resist any call for a complete test moratorium, and give no ground on the basic principle of curriculum-based tests, which are in theory and, as John Bishop has shown, also in fact the best route to improved quality and equity.

- Keep at least a few competency tests in reading, writing, and math. They should carry high stakes (but not unreasonably exalted cutoff points) so long as society agrees that our citizens need these competencies. Well-verified competency-based tests are like those little birds that tell us whether the air in the mine is safe. They reflect the reality principle in education by showing whether competence is truly being achieved.

In short, those states brave enough to have started down this path should continue and improve the policy of using curriculum-based tests, with the stakes gradually getting higher. This is the only known way of achieving the democratic ideal of making the school as effective educationally as the home. That is the appropriate norm by which content standards and tests should be measured in a democracy.

Those state tests, on the other hand, that are based on no specific content standards mainly increase anxiety without increasing learning. They are no better than commercially available competency tests; in fact, they are generally less fair and accurate. For profound theoretical reasons, these skills tests cannot help schools narrow the achievement gap between groups.

In states where good curriculum-based tests are built on good, specific content standards, the following can be predicted for current kindergartners and first graders. By grade 7 or 8, when the content-based curriculum has "diffused knowledge" (to use Jefferson's phrase) and has done much of its compensatory work, academic achievement will have risen for all groups. Higher scores on curriculum-based tests will be well-correlated with higher scores on competency-based tests, which will show a significant narrowing of the competency gap between groups. At that point we shall have moved closer to the ideal of a truly democratic system of education.

E. D. Hirsch Jr. is professor emeritus at the University of Virginia and founder of the Core Knowledge Foundation in Charlottesville, Virginia. He is author of numerous books, including *The Knowledge Deficit* (Houghton Mifflin, 2006), *Cultural Literacy: What Every American Needs to Know* (Houghton Mifflin, 1987), and *The Schools We Need and Why We Don't Have Them* (Anchor, 1999).

In the past 10 years, several developments have given momentum to the movement to use multiple measures—not just standardized tests—to evaluate student achievement. Rhode Island and New Hampshire have adopted competence-based systems in high school and recently met with five other states to share their experience. Small, innovative schools like those funded by the Bill & Melinda Gates Foundation rely on multiple measures to assess student performance. And there appears to be a growing backlash against standardized testing and the punitive accountability provisions of No Child Left Behind. A drop in the bucket? Yes, but an encouraging development.—RAW

PUBLISHED OCTOBER 13, 2004

MULTIPLE MEASURES

[RONALD A. WOLK]

America's obsession with standardized tests seems to intensify every year, especially now that the No Child Left Behind Act has raised the stakes by requiring that schools raise their test scores each year to avoid penalties and ultimately closure.

A longtime supporter of standards and accountability recently expressed his despair over the way standards-based reform has evolved: "I'm afraid we don't have standards-based reform anymore, so much as we have test-based reform."

Our almost total reliance on standardized test scores as a measure of school and student performance has become a powerful obstacle to reform and innovation. Because the test questions are based on the conventional curriculum and are designed to assess the acquisition of information, they reinforce the status quo and put pressure on teachers to teach strictly to the test.

Small, innovative schools, such as the models being supported by the Bill & Melinda Gates Foundation, concentrate on educating one student at a time by tailoring curricula and pedagogy to meet the needs and abilities of their students. Having to prepare their students to pass standardized tests compromises and stifles their innovative practices.

The foolish emphasis we put on testing is expensive, unnecessary, and probably harmful to millions of children.

Despite warnings from testing experts and educators that important decisions should not be based on a single measure, 24 states now require high school students to pass an exit exam to graduate or are planning to do so.

Standardized tests have too many deficiencies to be the determining factor in assessing student achievement, but their most egregious flaw is that they don't address the qualities and values that most parents want their children to have—the skills and attitudes needed to continue learning on their own and to be good citizens, productive workers, and fulfilled human beings. Parents want their children to develop virtues and values that we can all agree on, like diligence, honesty, tolerance, fairness, and compassion—none of which are assessed by standardized tests.

When I suggested to a friend who has worked at both the state and district levels that policymakers and educators should develop an assessment system of multiple measures to evaluate students' academic and personal achievement, he said it would be too complicated and subjective to be practical.

"The psychometricians would have a field day," he scoffed. "What would you include in the multiple measures? How would you assure that the measures are valid?" At that moment, I had no answers. But as I pondered the matter I became convinced that such a system is possible and, even with imperfections, would be superior to basing everything on test scores.

For the sake of argument, imagine an assessment system that requires 80 points out of a possible 135 to graduate. A student earning 100 to 115 points would graduate with honors, and those with more than 115 would receive high honors. Students could earn the points as follows:

- 40 points for passing the mandated state or district exit test.

- 0–20 points for the grade point average of all courses. An A average would earn 20 points; a B would earn 15; a C, 10; a D, 5.

- 0–25 points for personal work (such as exhibition in the arts and sciences), participation in class, and overall behavior. In written evaluations, two teachers would each rate the student on a scale of 0 to 25 points, and the student would be awarded the average.

- 10 points for having fewer than five unexcused absences.

- 0–25 points for participating and excelling in extracurricular activities. Students would receive 15 points for participating in two or more activities, and they could earn up to 5 additional points on the recommendation of the activity's adviser or coach, and another 5 points for an award received in the activity, like an athletic letter or a writing prize.

- 0 to 15 points for volunteer work in the community. The number of points earned would be based on the recommendation of the adult supervising the activity.

Students could not earn enough points to graduate just by passing the mandated exit test; they would have to show enough achievement on other important measures to earn 40 additional points. And students who did not pass the exit test could still earn a diploma, but only if they excelled on all of the other measures and earned 80 of the remaining 95 points. If a student who failed the exit test earned the maximum for extracurricular activities, volunteer work, and attendance, he or she would still need to earn 30 points in either grades or teacher evaluations.

These categories and point scales are offered as examples. A group of hardworking policymakers, educators, and parents could surely develop a better and more sophisticated assessment system of multiple measures.

Some of the evaluations are indeed subjective, but no more so than the evaluations students will face when they leave school and enter the real world. Few of us take standardized tests after we graduate. Instead, we are judged on what we produce and how we behave.

Teachers, advisers, and coaches evaluate students continuously, and their assessments should count for something in such an important decision as whether a student graduates or gets promoted.

The reason most often given for high stakes is to motivate students. That probably works for a portion of the students who are doing only as much as necessary to get by. For many others, high stakes probably encourage an early exit from school. Perhaps we could motivate both groups more effectively by awarding college scholarships to students who graduate with honors.

Ronald A. Wolk, founding editor of *Education Week,* is chairman of the board of Editorial Projects in Education, the newspaper's parent corporation. He lives in Warwick, Rhode Island. The views expressed in this essay are his own.

PART FOUR

CURRICULUM IN THE CLASSROOM

Yes, the more things change, the more they stay the same. My student teacher is at a middle school where teachers are organized in "teams of two." One teacher is responsible for social studies and literacy—just as I was as a "core teacher" in the 1960s. The new twist is a second "core" teacher for math and science. Cooperative learning lives as teachers work to create "classroom communities." But the mood swings continue. No Child Left Behind and the standards movement perhaps force too much attention on academics. Problems such as bullying and substance abuse affect student performance, but educators' efforts to make schools safer don't count. Low test scores should be just one measure of a failing school. Would the pendulum stop swinging if politicians and policymakers recognized that learning is inextricably linked to students' personal, social, emotional, and physical well-being?—AWD

PUBLISHED JUNE 9, 1993

CURRICULUM MOOD SWINGS

[ANNE WESCOTT DODD]

I noticed a call for manuscripts on "The Changing Curriculum" in an educational journal and thought, "Hmm. That should be an interesting issue, now that so many schools are involved in restructuring." Later, however, as I remembered my own career in education, I realized that the truest statement I could make about change in schools is, "The more things change, the more they stay the same."

I know from the work of Michael Fullan and others who have explored the complex factors involved in the initiation, implementation, and continuation of a change that instituting lasting change is difficult and elusive. Yet the title for a new bibliography from the National Association for Core Curriculum—*Research on the Effectiveness of Block-Time, Course, and Interdisciplinary Team Teaching Programs*—led me to wonder if there has been any real change in curriculum since the early 1960s.

The word *core* in the association's name instantly brought back memories of my days as a beginning teacher in California in the early 1960s. I was hired to teach English and social studies in a junior high school, but since we were all assigned to teach the same group of students for two periods, we were called *core teachers*. We talked about *core classes,* not English and social studies.

At the time I was too busy as a novice teacher trying to prevent chaos in my classes to consider the theoretical basis for the district's curriculum policies, so I do not know what arguments persuaded district administrators to create the core classes. Perhaps they were similar to those being put forth today: subjects should be integrated because real-world problems are interdisciplinary, for example; or 45-minute periods are not conducive to interactive student learning and reflection. I do recall that we were encouraged to have students do projects that combined English and social studies and to involve them in writing for social studies as well as for English.

Even though *team teaching* and *collaboration* were not discussed, there was a natural basis for teacher collaboration. Because each teacher taught five periods rather than six, we each had one split class. Although one teacher opted to teach English while the other took responsibility for social studies, it made sense for us to coordinate our teaching. We were dealing with the same group of students and taught both subjects to our other students.

When I left that district five years later, though, core—and along with it, much of the informal teacher collaboration—was dead. I'm not sure exactly when or why administrators began scheduling the two subjects as separate classes—to facilitate developing the master schedule maybe. My last year in that junior high I was an "English teacher," and my friend, a "social-studies teacher." The junior high where I taught next had never even jumped on the "core bandwagon."

Like the phoenix rising from the ashes, however, reforms that die are often reborn, albeit dressed in slightly different feathers. What counts as an innovation may not be new but rather newly rediscovered. By the early '70s educational reform was in high gear, and while some of the innovations, such as elective courses, seemed on the surface to have split the curriculum up into many tiny fragments, that wasn't always the case. Many electives were interdisciplinary—filmmaking and humanities courses, for example. And teachers were teaching in teams. In the small rural high school where I was then teaching, the three of us who made up the English department developed a new curriculum and team-taught the freshman students in heterogeneous classes.

Because the school also instituted a flexible modular schedule, teachers had the option of scheduling students not only in longer blocks of time but also in groups of varying sizes for different purposes. In my short-story course, for instance, all the students met as a large group for an hour, during which general information about short stories was presented and discussed. Then, as a follow-up, there were 40-minute small-group discussion sessions. Students in each of these groups read different stories, depending on their interest and reading level. In the small-group sessions, the students and I talked about the particular stories they had read in relation to the material introduced to all students in the large-group meeting. The modular schedule made it possible to eliminate the rigidly tracked classes that are still the norm in most high schools and one of the targets of current reform.

Modular scheduling also provided teachers with time during the school day to work on curriculum. Because teachers had more unscheduled time with the modular schedule than is the case with a traditional one, we met frequently to discuss professional concerns and develop curricula. A colleague and I designed and team-taught several elective courses. It was also easy to schedule one-on-one individual or small-group sessions for students who needed extra help. Moreover, we often became unofficial "teacher advisers" for some students, since the changes in the schedule created a climate that encouraged a great deal of informal conversation between teachers and students.

But these innovations did not last, and I was moved to write an article about the benefits of the flexible modular schedule in that school and its unfortunate demise. That year, the most rewarding of my entire career in education, I experienced and came to value many of the "innovations" that have become part of the restructuring movement today. Even though I now understand more clearly the complex political and organizational factors that killed our efforts to change that rural school, it doesn't ease my sense of loss.

Of course my school wasn't the only one to return to traditional ways of educating students. Things changed on the national scene as well. The back-to-basics movement of the late 1970s and early 1980s led to the re-institution of the usual year-long courses and increased demands for accountability. Teachers pressured to increase student scores on standardized tests didn't have the encouragement or energy to develop interdisciplinary courses or student projects.

Curriculum and classroom practice are much like the weather in Maine: if you don't like it, wait a minute. As reform has elided into restructuring, teachers have once again been asked to think about change. The concepts aren't new, but some of the labels are. *Collaborative* or *cooperative learning* seems a lot like *small-group training* in the 1970s. *Block scheduling* might be thought of as a less flexible variation of the *modular schedule.* Take a journey back through the history of American education with Lawrence Cremin or Herbert Kliebard and it is easy to trace the complex pattern created as political and social movements caused the dominance of one curriculum vision or another to wax and wane. It is also clear that the current movement to institute a more student-centered, interactive, and integrated curriculum has its roots in John Dewey's idea of education as experience.

Despite the introduction of computers and other responses to changes in the outside world, schools today still teach much of the same basic content they did decades ago. Arthur Applebee, for instance, who conducted a study in U.S. secondary schools to compare required book-length works in the curriculum today with those in 1963, found that there were very few differences. Furthermore, there was a surprising degree of agreement among public, Catholic, and private schools. Plays of Shakespeare—*Romeo and Juliet, Hamlet, Macbeth,* and *Julius Caesar*—still top the list. The authors of the top 10 titles in 1989 as in 1963 include only one female (Harper Lee, *To Kill a Mockingbird)* and no minority authors. Applebee does note that works by women and minorities have been added to the curriculum in some schools.

His findings reinforce my own personal impression that much remains unchanged. Every time I have scored open-ended-response essays written by students for the English composition test or the Advanced Placement test in English, I have been struck by how many of the books students choose to write about are the same ones I read as a student and taught as a beginning teacher. As I have observed classrooms at all levels, I have been amazed at how much time some teachers spend on grammar worksheets and vocabulary lists, despite a vast amount of research suggesting that teaching skills in isolation is not effective.

What is really sad—and probably inescapable—is that young teachers today will invest as much energy and enthusiasm in making changes as I once did only to see the national mood swing back again. The changes they make in their own teaching will stay with them because they will be forever changed by what they have learned and experienced with their students. They may, however, soon find it increasingly difficult to teach in ways they believe are right and true. When the public demands that schools once again return to the old ways of doing things, teachers and administrators will be forced to respond, and the climate will be very unfriendly for those who believe in a student-centered experiential curriculum.

Some might argue that curriculum change today is more research-based than it was in the past, but still I wonder. Changing curriculum? So what else is new? Like ocean tides that ebb and flow, so too goes curriculum. The more things change, the more they remain the same. Perhaps the curriculum question we most need to ask and answer is not *What?* but *Why?*

Anne Wescott Dodd is senior lecturer in education at Bates College in Lewiston, Maine. Her most recent books are *How Communities Build Stronger Schools* (Palgrave-Macmillan, 2002) and *Making Our High Schools Better* (St. Martin's Press, 1999), both co-authored with Jean L. Konzal.

My views have not changed fundamentally with regard to the neglect of the arts in present-day "reform" proposals. However, the various reports to which I referred in my essay now seem to have congealed into the far more prescriptive and controlling No Child Left Behind policy. There have been proposals for support of arts education, often supported by the claim that it strengthens subject-matter learning. Not believing that the arts have to be justified in such a pragmatic fashion, I would argue all the more forcefully that art experiences hold a promise of overcoming the apathy that troubles so many of us at this time of war, torture, genocide, and interference with free speech. I would repeat what I said about passion and imagination and say even more about the values of pleasure and delight, both of which may infuse experiences with the arts.—MG

PUBLISHED FEBRUARY 19, 1997

WHY IGNORE THE FORMS OF ART?

[MAXINE GREENE]

The voices calling for a reform of teacher education are multiple and diverse. Perhaps the most far-ranging and persuasive is the report of the National Commission on Teaching and America's Future, *What Matters Most: Teaching for America's Future*. But the teachers' unions, the National Council for Accreditation of Teacher Education, the Council of Chief State School Officers, and a number of schools of education are making their own contributions. Certainly critics of the schools like E. D. Hirsch Jr., head of the Core

Knowledge Foundation and author of *The Schools We Need and Why We Don't Have Them,* put much of the onus for what is wrong upon teacher education and are articulating their own proposals for reform and change.

It is difficult, nearly impossible, to take issue with people who speak so eloquently about quality, excellence, equity, collaboration, care, and professional development. There can be no disagreement on the need to educate all of America's children for a changing world and for the technological revolution; nor can there be disagreement on the need for teachers with the knowledge and skills required to enable all children to learn. "We must reclaim the soul of America," wrote the authors of the National Commission's report. "And to do so, we need an education system that helps people to forge shared values, to understand and respect other perspectives, to learn and work at high levels of competence, to take risks and persevere against the odds, to work comfortably with people from diverse backgrounds, and to continue to learn throughout life."

Reading that, noting the "human core" that presumably must be attended to, I am startled by the ignoring of the arts and the traditions and conversations out of which they emerge. I do not mean only exploration of various media for the sake of self-expression, important as this may be. I mean the great range of artworks that mark the high points of cultures developing over the centuries. I mean what Clifford Geertz, in his book *Local Culture,* calls "art as a cultural system," the ways in which the arts exemplify the sense of being-in-the-world. To study an art form, writes Geertz, is to study a sensibility and to realize "that such a sensibility is essentially a collective formation, and that the foundations of such a formation are as wide as social existence and as deep."

Teachers provided with access to "high-quality professional development" ought not be deprived of opportunities to engage with sensibilities in Clifford Geertz's sense.

But there is another aspect of the study of art forms that not only awakens teachers to all sorts of new perspectives on the lived world, past and present, but also provides occasions for authentic active learning of the kind that is paradigmatic for the learning that excellent teachers are supposed to make possible for the young. To enter, for example, a Cezanne landscape, to learn to "read" that landscape, requires a mode of reflectiveness and imaginative play seldom experienced outside the domains of the art. Cezanne, like Herman Melville and Toni Morrison, like Martha Graham and Twyla Tharp, like Arthur Miller and Terrence McNally, created out of his own substance and craft and experience works that can be brought alive only for people willing to lend them their lives, to infuse them with their own awareness and their own imaginative energy.

Personal agency, passion, imagination, and a making of meaning: all of these must be part of full engagement with the arts, and it is difficult to accept a call for excellent teaching and "teaching for America's future" that pays no heed to the awakenings the arts make possible, the breaking with what Virginia Woolf called the "cotton wool of daily life." To teach for the future requires a break from the routine and the ordinary, from the merely repetitive. And the arts, of all forms, may awaken teachers-to-be from the "anesthetic" and provide opportunities for them to choose themselves through the projects of their teaching, through their being in the world.

I choose to end with a few lines written by John Dewey in his book *The Public and Its Problems*. The conscious life of opinion and judgment, he said, "often proceeds on a superficial and trivial plane. But their lives reach a deeper level. The function of art has always been to break through the crust of conventionalized and routine consciousness. . . . Artists have always been the real purveyors of news, for it is not the outward happening in itself which is new, but the kindling by it of emotion, perception, and appreciation."

My argument is not so much with reformers' emphasis on technology and the economy. It is not with the instances of teaching presented. It is certainly not with the moral values noted here and there, nor with the commitment to democracy. It is with the all-too-familiar dismissal of the arts, as if they are frills, as if they do not matter, as if they were not central to our understanding of the culture and of ourselves.

Maxine Greene is professor emeritus of philosophy and education at Teachers College, Columbia University, in New York City. She is also professor-in-residence at the Lincoln Center Institute for the Arts in Education and past president of the American Educational Research Association and the Philosophy of Education Society.

Why the continuing reading crisis? Our schools are out of touch with the times. They haven't made the leap into this astonishing information age. Reading was not a job-essential skill for the farmers or factory workers or blue-collar workers who dominated the workforce just a few decades ago. So, mostly, schools taught reading as a skill meant to enrich your life (which it does). Literature meant novels or short stories. But in this new age all the good jobs demand analytical reading skills. They are best taught using today's literary form: nonfiction. Teach language arts with well-written history or science and you'll see reading scores soar.—JH

PUBLISHED NOVEMBER 21, 2001

RESCUE THE WONDER OF THE PRINTED PAGE

[JOY HAKIM]

I visit schools across the nation and, again and again, they strike me as anti-reading places. Many of the teachers I see, who have the best of intentions, seem actually to be keeping children from reading. I was speaking to a group of reading instructors in Virginia and that was the message I brought them. Some in my audience looked as if they were searching for rotten tomatoes. If they'd found any, they might have pelted me.

But I've spent a lot of time in classrooms, and I'll stick with that statement.

It's not that I am unimpressed with the teachers I see. Quite the contrary. Wherever I am I find terrific teachers. Intelligent men and women dedicated to their profession. Teachers who spend their own money on classroom supplies. Teachers who care with all their beings about their students and about education and who usually are appreciated, deservedly, by parents and students.

Yet something is wrong. There's a kind of reverse synergy at work in our schools. The total is less than the sum of the parts. And teachers as well as children are victims.

As to reading? We've had years and years of reading initiatives. Our schools are obsessed with reading scores. We've neglected most of the other subjects to concentrate on reading drills. And what has it gotten us? Third grade reading scores have inched up, but everyone in the field knows that it is in fourth grade that solid subject matter is introduced and many of our youngsters can't handle that key to success in the Information Age.

University of Virginia educator E. D. Hirsch Jr. says that the fourth grade reading gap between rich and poor, which widens in each succeeding grade, "represents the single greatest failure in American public schooling and the most disheartening affront to the ideal of democratic education." This year, for the third straight year, nearly half of New York's eighth graders failed a state reading exam.

What we aren't doing in schools is exciting children with the printed page and the wonders it can offer. We continue to present reading as a boring school subject that can't compete with television. Yet as any reader will tell you, it is TV that is ultimately boring, and books are what can transport you to other worlds.

What's wrong? Some educators blame kids. Some blame today's families. Some say it's societal values. But spend time in many of today's schools and I think you'll see what I see: practices that inhibit subject-matter reading. Why?

Partly it's curricula overloaded with trivia. Partly it's an anti-intellectual bias that pervades many schools of education, the very places we should find support for thinking subjects. And that leads to numbing overdoses of methodology at the expense of "real" subjects. In my home state of Colorado it has led the legislature to decree that majors in chemistry, classics, Spanish, or fine arts are not acceptable for an elementary school teacher.

Perhaps even more important, we've let manufactured commercial textbooks determine school curricula and keep real books from children. If we want our children to read we need to give them books worth reading. Check out your child's textbooks. The graphics may be impressive, but see if you can find a book that is a page-turner. Very few are written, as most good books are, by a single author.

School reading is still mostly taught from readers with disconnected stories and excerpts chopped from books that children could easily read whole. And a disproportionate amount of time is spent on reading skills rather than on reading itself. That approach hasn't worked.

Why not all of *Wind in the Willows* rather than the out-of-context chapter found in one text I've seen? Is it habit, or sales pressure from the multibillion-dollar textbook industry? Whatever, it doesn't make much sense. Kids are smarter than the books we give them.

There are wonderful exceptions. In a second grade classroom I visited in Virginia a few years ago, each child was reading a real book and keeping a journal of his or her reading. Quietly, one by one, boys and girls went to the teacher's desk for private reading sessions. The children in that class—each reading at his or her own level—were averaging a book a week.

That same teacher divided her class into traditional groups for a reading-skills instruction period—pointedly separate from the very popular and productive reading time. In oral book reports, children shared their books with their classmates.

These kids were reading mostly library books, not disjointed textbooks. Their reading scores were well above average in an urban public school. Even better, they were learning that authors write books so that one chapter logically follows another. And that good books have underlying themes and ideas.

I admit to a vested interest in this subject. I'm the author of a narrative history of the United States being used in schools across the country. I wrote those books to teach reading, as well as history and civic values and geography and all the important things the subject can address.

But what happens to those books in some schools? I see teachers extracting chapters, or sometimes even paragraphs. They assume kids can't read books—even small books—and without meaning to they encourage snippet reading. Many do something else: they summarize the reading for their students, thus eliminating any need for their students actually to read for themselves. It leads to something the experts call "fake" reading.

It's all done with good intentions, and often a sense of desperation. The kids don't read well, so we have to help them along, and pretty soon the teacher is doing all the work.

There was a time when it did not matter much if you were an efficient reader or not; today it does.

We're losing young minds. Too many of our youngsters are functionally illiterate, too many others can't do Information Age reading. In the school world, reading and literature are still seen, most often, as ventures into fiction. But today's adult reading is mostly nonfiction. And reading nonfiction takes very different skills than reading fiction.

Which makes content subjects like history and science ideal for teaching 21st-century reading. With them you get a double whammy: you teach kids subject matter and you teach them to read analytically. It's time to recognize the importance of critical reading, not to abandon those subjects that rely on it.

Few subjects resonate with children as good history does—it's the story of real people and real adventures—but that has been lost in the dull litany of facts that is standard social studies fare. The result is a historically illiterate population, along with generations of poor readers.

Given the tedious, committee-written commercial textbooks, it's no surprise that history has been neglected as a way to teach reading. That it includes great stories—ones that just happen to be true—is rarely considered.

I know firsthand that you can teach reading using challenging, action-filled nonfiction—especially history told as a narrative and science presented as a quest—and that it resonates with today's information-hungry kids. But that concept isn't recognized in many schools. It's time to reconsider. The way we've been doing it hasn't worked.

Joy Hakim is author of *A History of US* (3rd ed., Oxford University Press, 2002), a 10-volume American history series for children, and the first recipient of the James A. Michener Award in Writing from the National Council for the Social Studies. Hakim is now writing the *Story of Science* series for the Smithsonian Institution: *Aristotle Leads the Way* and *Newton at the Center* have been published; *Einstein Adds a New Dimension* is scheduled for 2007. All of her books are intended to teach critical reading as well as subject matter.

Even revisiting this piece four years later, my feelings about this topic haven't changed at all; in fact, if anything, they've grown stronger. Children need the time to be children, but our punitive testing regime and the scores of "drill and kill" curricula being forced on inner-city kids are doing their best to banish whimsy from the classroom. I hope more school districts will choose in the future to be gentle with their students and allow their fascination to grow into creativity, and curiosity, and knowledge.—JDE

PUBLISHED JUNE 12, 2002

IN DEFENSE OF WHIMSY

[JANE DIMYAN-EHRENFELD]

Without exception, the best conversations I've had with any of the elementary school students I've taught have always been the ones I'm not really supposed to be having. Nowhere in the Boston Standards of Learning does it say that I'm to teach my first grade students the origins of the names of the days of the week, but when they asked about this one morning I couldn't help tabling a lesson on sentence structure to give them some answers. I told them what I knew—Saturday is named for Saturn, Wednesday for Woden, Monday is the moon's day, and Sunday is the sun's day—and then gave a short overview of mythology to tide them over until I could research the rest.

I'm glad I digressed; if I hadn't, I doubt Christopher ever would have asked me his question, the one that would have stumped a roomful of philosophers. He asked, "Ms. Ehrenfeld, if people believe in the gods, do the gods believe in people?" Hard to get a question like that when you're drilling them on the appropriate placement of capital letters.

Not all of my conversations with my students lead to the kinds of questions that leave me speechless or sleepless; some conversations are purely silly, some are ethical debates, some are just brief speculations on a small but significant topic of interest. And sometimes it's not even a conversation that transforms my classroom into someplace mystical; it's just a moment or a mood that appears out of nowhere and disappears immediately unless noticed. Yet all of these times are essential to the kind of classroom I want to create for the children—the kind of classroom where the paths we travel are sometimes mine and sometimes theirs, where their curiosity is given as much space as they need it to have, as much air as they need for their exploration of the world to survive.

Creating this world for the children also means sometimes accepting that I won't be able to follow all the startling twists and bends of their seemingly illogical logic, or that when I do finally figure out what they're saying, the conversation may be long finished and forgotten.

This happens to me one day in December, in my first grade classroom, as I am getting ready to start my morning meeting with the children. I look down at Nequan, seated on a pillow just in front of my rocking chair, and notice that the pillow is strewn with tiny white crystals of some unknown substance. *Great,* I think, *it's not bad enough they give me their colds and flus and rashes, now they're bringing me anthrax?*

I look at Nequan, who grins up at me. "Nequan," I ask, "what is all over that pillow?"

Nequan shrugs, his grin suddenly shadowed by just a hint of guilt.

I give him my best FBI interrogation look and ask again: "What is on the pillow?"

Another shrug. "Sugar?" he tries, clearly hoping I'll be satisfied with this and move on to the "Good Morning Song." No such luck.

"Where did it come from?"

By now the guilty look has completely eclipsed the grin. "My pocket?"

"Your pocket?"

He does a quick check, then affirms his answer: "My pocket."

"How did it get there?"

He thinks. "It fell in?" He looks up at me quickly, trying to see if I'll buy that answer.

"Nequan, sugar does not just fall into your pocket. How did it get there?"

"I put it in?"

"Why on Earth did you put sugar in your pocket?"

Just a hint of a shrug this time, then a more assertive answer: "For my raisins."

Do I want to keep asking him questions? I'm starting to feel as if I've lost control of the conversation completely.

"Do you have raisins in your pocket?"

"Nope."

"Did you bring raisins to school today?"

"Nope."

"So why do you have sugar in your pocket?"

"For my raisins!"

I give up. Complete, unconditional surrender. I tell him to clean the sugar off the pillow and clean out his pockets, then we continue with the morning meeting.

Baffled for days by this conversation, I finally figure out the reason for Nequan's sugary pockets. We had been on a field trip the day before I caught him with the sugar, and the cafeteria had packed boxes of raisins in the children's lunches. Nequan, who clearly likes his raisins with sugar, had been obliged to eat them plain. The next morning, determined not to let the possibility of raisins for lunch catch him unprepared, he had filled his pockets with sugar before school. Had I been six, perhaps I would have understood this immediately, but during the conversation, my slow, clumsy adult brain just couldn't keep up with his logic.

The fact that rigid connections and pathways have not yet been burned into these children's minds also means that they write some of the most moving and original poetry I've ever read. A third grader, recounting her bout of the flu, writes, "I shut the door/I saw the bandit of paradise/I knew/this would happen/to my body/blooming like the sun/when I got sick." Another, creating a fictitious character in a poem, writes, "She has/keys in her/back pocket/she dreamed/she had/puppies on/the step/drinking /milk/out of/ the sky." A third, angry for no reason she will ever tell us, suddenly reveals herself in this poem:

> One day I
> saw two ugly persons.
> I didn't know it was my mother.
> She had brown eyes and brown hair.
> You
> all
> know it
> was my mother.
> The next thing
> I saw
> was an
> ugly man he
> had black eyes
> black and gray hair.
> You all
> know
> it
> was
> my father.

The two months I spend every spring teaching them poetry and letting them run down its corridors without restraints of any kind is not in any of the curricula I've ever been handed, but those months are always the time when I learn more about them than I've ever known, and when they do their most creative and astonishing work.

I am not a Montessori teacher, neither do I work in middle- or upper-class progressive schools. I have taught only inner-city children in public schools where the standardized-test pressure is intense, and the sense that there is little time to waste if we want our students to catch up with their wealthier, whiter peers pervades everything we do. There are many people—teachers, educational "experts," politicians, school administrators—who would say that two months of poetry, a morning spent discussing Greek and Roman mythology, even a short and mystifying conversation with a student are all stealing valuable time from the curriculum. But I honor my students too much to believe that every minute of school time should be spent thinking in the narrow ways that a curriculum writer far away in an office has determined they should think.

My classroom is a far better place when I listen to my children: to a question I have never imagined, a request for information that is not going to be on any test but that they just want to know because they are curious and at this very moment it is important, or to a conversation that leaves me puzzled but sometime later opens a window into the way they think, and in turn makes me a better teacher for them. Most of all, I won't be responsible for hurrying my children out of that age when so many things are interesting and so much is new, and when their desire to learn is pure and not corrupted by the rewards we offer and the punishments we threaten if they do not learn what we want them to learn when we want them to learn it.

All of this should not be taken to mean that we spend all day in my classroom carelessly chatting about whatever pops into my students' minds. We work very hard: my children have learned to read this year, they are good at math, they've learned some history and some science too. It's just this: if at the end of the day I find Reginald standing at the window instead of reading at his seat and I see that he is wide-eyed and absolutely entranced by a squirrel in a tree in the yard, I will not call to him to sit down and pick up his book. In fact, I might even join him there for a moment and remember what it feels like to be amazed by a squirrel.

After this essay was published, Jane Dimyan-Ehrenfeld taught for four more years at the same school, located in the Roxbury section of Boston. She taught first grade, third grade, and fourth grade, with the result that she had many of the same students in her class for three years. After her fifth year at the school she made the difficult decision to leave teaching to pursue a career in education law. She is now a first-year law student at Georgetown University Law Center. She is a Public Interest Law Scholar at the Center and aims to use her degree to work on desegregation and other equity issues in education. She misses her students terribly but feels better knowing that she will, she hopes, have the chance to change the way education works for many children in America.

PART FIVE

TECHNOLOGY AND LEARNING

Fig. 58.

"We are concerned that black people master the new form of literacy.
We want these programs to serve as digital bridges."—Statement by Henry
Louis Gates Jr. in an article in the *Harvard Crimson*, October 10, 2000, on the launch
of a new after-school program sponsored by Harvard University's W.E.B. Du Bois
Institute for African and African American Research. The program aimed to teach
young people in a low-income neighborhood in Boston about the Internet
using content focused on black history and culture.

PUBLISHED JANUARY 12, 2000

BLACK TO THE FUTURE

[HENRY LOUIS GATES JR.]

Following the Stono Rebellion of 1739 in South Carolina, the largest uprising
of slaves in the colonies before the American Revolution, legislators there responded by banishing two forms of literacy crucial to the slaves: the mastery
of letters and the mastery of talking drums. Both forms of literacy had been
pivotal to the slaves' capacity to rebel.

For the next century and a half, then, access to literacy became for the
slaves a hallmark of their humanity and a tool to their own liberation, a liberation of the spirit as well as the body. The relation between freedom and
literacy became the compelling theme of the slave narratives, the great
body of printed books that ex-slaves generated to pronounce their common

This Commentary marked the first in an occasional series of "2000 & Beyond" essays. The
Carnegie Corporation of New York and the Ford Foundation provided funding for the series.

humanity with white Americans and to indict the system that had oppressed them. In the century and a third since the abolition of slavery, the possession of literacy—mastering the master's tools to dismantle, or reconstruct, the master's house—has been a cardinal value of the African American tradition. It is no accident that the first great victory in the legal battle over segregation was fought on the grounds of education, of equal access to literacy.

Today, however, blacks are facing a new form of denial to the tools of literacy, this time in the guise of access to the digital-knowledge economy. And while the dilemma that our ancestors so passionately confronted was imposed by others, this form of cybersegregation is, to a surprising degree, self-imposed.

The government's latest attempt to understand why low-income African Americans and Hispanics are slower to embrace the Internet and the personal computer than whites—the recent U.S. Department of Commerce study *Falling Through the Net*—suggests that income alone can't be blamed for the so-called "digital divide." For example, among families earning $15,000 to $35,000 annually, more than 33 percent of whites own computers, compared with only 19 percent of African Americans—a gap that has widened by 64 percent over the past five years despite declining computer prices.

These implications go far beyond online trading and chat rooms. Net promoters nationwide are right to be concerned that the digital divide threatens to become a 21st-century poll tax that, de facto, disenfranchises a third of the nation. Our children, especially, need access not only to the vast resources that technology offers for education, but also to the multicultural context that defines their place in the world. Today we stand at the brink of becoming two societies, one largely white and plugged in, the other black and unplugged.

One of the most tragic aspects of slavery was its devastating effectiveness at severing social connections. In a process that sociologist Orlando Patterson calls "social death," slavery sought to disconnect blacks from their history and culture, from family ties and a sense of community. De jure segregation, following the Civil War, sought to disconnect blacks from equal economic opportunity, from the network of social contacts that enable upward mobility, and indeed from the broader world of ideas.

As the black middle class has grown so dramatically since the onset of affirmative action in the late 1960s, new forms of disconnectedness have afflicted the black community. Middle-class professionals often feel socially and culturally isolated from their white peers, at work and in their neighborhoods, and from their black peers left behind in the underclass. For their part, the children of the black underclass often lack middle-class role models to help them connect to ideas, to an awareness of our people's past so that they can draw a sense of identity from the accomplishments of our history and culture, to role models they can emulate, to mentors and peers who share their interests and can help facilitate their goals, and to the crucial capacity to express ideas and receive feedback, a process that develops analytical skills.

The Clinton administration is determined to see that every school system in the nation has access to the World Wide Web. Providing online access for all Americans regardless of income is surely part of the structural answer to this digital divide. But the Commerce Department study suggests that the solution will require more than cheap PCs, as crucial as this is.

One possible solution is the content of the information available on the Internet. Until recently, the African American presence on the Internet was minimal, reflecting the chicken-and-egg nature of online economics. Despite sites such as Black Voices and Afronet, relatively few investors have been willing to fund sites appealing to a PC-scarce community. (A notable exception is Black Entertainment Television's soon-to-be-launched portal, backed with $35 million by Liberty Digital, News Corporation, USA Networks, and Microsoft.) Few African Americans have been compelled to sign on to a medium that offers little to interest them. And educators have repeatedly raised concerns about the lack of strong technology-based educational resources for multicultural education.

The problem is somewhat analogous to the birth of the recording industry in the 1920s. Blacks began to respond to this new medium only when mainstream companies such as Columbia Records introduced "race records"—blues and jazz disks targeted at a nascent black market. Blacks who would never have dreamed of spending hard-earned money for a record by Rudy Vallee or Kate Smith would stand in lines several blocks long to purchase the new Bessie Smith or Duke Ellington hit. New content made the new medium attractive. The growth of Web sites dedicated to the interests and needs of black consumers can play the same role for the Web that race records did for the recording industry.

But even targeted content can only go so far. More and more scholars are admitting that the causes of poverty are both structural and behavioral. And it is the behavioral aspect of this failure to utilize the tremendous opportunities Internet access affords that blacks themselves are best able to address.

We need a revolution in our people's attitudes toward education, in the literal sense of that word's etymology, which suggests a return. When we were growing up in the 1950s, the blackest thing we could aspire to be was a lawyer like Thurgood Marshall, an educator like Mary McLeod Bethune, or a doctor like Charles Drew. And while we reveled in the achievements in the arena, on the court, and on the playing field of heroes such as Sugar Ray Robinson, Althea Gibson, and Willie Mays, and lived and died with their victories and defeats, we were taught that the serious business of civil rights demanded of us a commitment to excellence in the classroom.

Far too many of our children have lost this determination to fight racism, at all costs, against the odds, by acquiring knowledge, a passion that fired our generation. Far too many believe it easier to become a professional athlete than a member of a profession such as law or medicine, when statistically the reverse is true. There are far more Vernon Jordans than Michael Jordans—by a factor of 10—but we often act as if the reverse were true.

And a large part of the responsibility to reverse this dangerous and debilitating tendency must be borne by blacks ourselves. As other ethnic groups have done in this country, we must develop community-generated after-school programs that supplement public education by teaching the history and culture of our own people and information technology.

Drawing upon corporate and foundation support, we can transform available facilities in the legion of churches, mosques, and community centers in our inner cities into after-school programs that focus on redressing the digital divide and teaching black history, drawing upon the many examples of black achievement in highly structured classes to reestablish a sense of social connection with our community's triumphant past. This in turn could very well regenerate the love of learning that was at the heart of both the abolitionist and the civil rights movements.

The Internet is the 21st century's talking drum, a high-tech "grapevine," the very kind of grassroots communication that has been such a powerful source of education and culture for our people since slavery. But this talking drum we have not yet learned to play.

Make no mistake about it: unless we utilize the new information technology to build and deepen the forms of social connection that slavery, a century of segregation, and subsequent class divisions within the black community have severed, African Americans will face a form of cybersegregation in the coming century just as devastating to the aspirations of the black community in its way as Jim Crow segregation was to our ancestors. But this time, the fault will be our own.

Henry Louis Gates Jr. is W.E.B. Du Bois Professor of the Humanities and director of the W.E.B. Du Bois Institute for African and African American Research at Harvard University. He is also coeditor with K. Anthony Appiah of the Encarta Africana encyclopedia published on CD-ROM by Microsoft (1999) and in book form by Basic Civitas Books under the title *Africana: The Encyclopedia of the African and African American Experience* (1999).

The puzzle of limited classroom use of new machines amid a river of technology money that I wrote about nearly a decade ago I subsequently answered in "Oversold and Underused: Computers in the Classroom." The many purposes of tax-supported public schools, the century-old age-graded school, and the constant demands on public schools to solve national problems by bolstering the economy, decreasing social inequalities, reducing obesity, and increasing patriotism explain the limited use of new technologies in classrooms by teachers and students. Goals, structures, and external demands influence classroom practice. So it was then, so it is now.—LC

PUBLISHED AUGUST 4, 1999

THE TECHNOLOGY PUZZLE

[LARRY CUBAN]

Here's a puzzle for both cheerleaders and skeptics of using new technologies in the classroom. Out of every ten teachers in this country, fewer than two are serious users of computers and other information technologies in their classrooms (several times a week); three to four are occasional users (about once a month); and the rest—four to five teachers out of every ten—never use the machines at all. When the type of classroom use is examined, we find that these powerful technologies end up being used most often for word processing and low-end applications. And this is after a decade of increases in access to computers, Internet capability, and purchases of software. In other organizations (think hospitals, major corporations, supermarkets), computer use is ubiquitous. Not so in schools.

How can this phenomenon of infrequent, low-end use of technology be occurring in our schools? For experts, there is no puzzle to be solved. The answers are straightforward and all point to teachers: their insufficient preparation in universities, their lack of specific training, too little time to learn, too many older teachers, "technophobia," and so on, ad infinitum. Surely, some of these scattershot explanations have merit in attempting to understand the paradox of increasing access and infrequent use.

What is missing from these neatly packaged reasons, however, is one over-looked fact: of those same ten American teachers, about seven have computers at home and use them to prepare lessons, communicate with colleagues and friends, search the Internet, and conduct personal business. In short, most teachers use computers at home more than at school. No technophobes here.

It is this fact that creates the puzzle of limited classroom use of new machines amid a river of technology money. It is this fact too that drives me to examine other reasons for the disparity, reasons seldom voiced in the media by either promoters or skeptics. The five areas that follow may offer explanations of the puzzle and broaden the debate over teachers' use of new technologies.

• *Contradictory advice from experts.* For almost two decades, experts hired by corporate vendors and entrepreneurial academics have exhorted teachers, particularly those in high schools, to use new technologies in their classrooms. Teachers must use the new, information-rich machines, they say, so that students will learn more, faster, and better to be prepared for the 21st century's knowledge-based workplace. But exactly what have these self-appointed experts told teachers about how computers should be used in schools?

When desktop computers began to appear in schools in the early 1980s, corporate leaders urged high school teachers to get their students "computer literate." The phrase then meant learning how to write BASIC programs. Experts said that learning to program would prepare students to think clearly and get jobs. Computer-savvy teachers who had learned BASIC on their own plunged into the task of teaching the language in newly established computer labs.

By the late 1980s, however, BASIC had disappeared. Now, freshly minted experts prodded high school teachers to teach computer applications (for example, word processing, spreadsheets, use of databases) because computers were analytic tools and, in the work world, knowing these applications paid off. Districts invested in more labs, more teachers were trained, and students began taking required courses in keyboarding and learning software applications that were used in the workplace.

By the mid-1990s, the prevailing wisdom among experts had shifted and computer literacy took on new meanings. Teachers were now asked to integrate the new technologies into their daily classroom routines by placing four to six new machines in each teacher's classroom rather than sending students to computer labs. Teachers were urged to learn and teach hypertext programming, or HTML, to help their students create multimedia products for an audience. Experts and their allies now said that students who were computer literate knew how to do research on the Internet, communicate via e-mail, and create their own World Wide Web pages. A series of so-called 'Net Days advertised the importance of wiring schools for the Internet, so that students could become part of the real world each and every day.

So, for the last two decades, experts have urged upon teachers an ever-shifting menu of advice: Teach BASIC. Teach HTML. Teach skills of using the Internet, e-mail, and producing multimedia projects. Teach applications relevant to the constantly changing workplace.

Now, let's imagine a couple of average high school teachers in the heart of Silicon Valley who have been around for these years of shifting advice and are eager to help their students learn. They have taken courses on using software applications that their district offers. They have bought computers and use them at home extensively to prepare lessons, record grades, and search the Internet for lessons they could use in their classes. They are enthusiastic about using computers with their students. They have listened to the experts; but since the advice keeps changing, they have largely ignored the wisdom of the moment. What gives them pause is not the experts' contradictions but other factors.

• *Intractable working conditions.* Although information technologies have transformed most corporate workplaces, our teachers' schedules and working conditions have changed very little. They teach five classes a day, each 50 to 55 minutes long. Their five classes contain at least three different preparations; that is, for the math teacher among our five, there are two classes of introductory algebra, two of geometry, and one calculus class. In those five classes, she sees 140 students a day. Colleagues in other districts, depending on how affluent the district is and how determined the school board and superintendent are to keep class size down, may see 125 to 175 students a day.

Or take the English teacher in our group, who assigns an essay in three of his ninth grade composition classes and for his two senior classes asks the students to answer five questions on *Hamlet*. He will face the prospect of reading and correcting 130 papers for students who expect their homework to be returned earlier rather than later. Like all high school teachers, he has at least one period a day set aside for planning lessons, seeing students, marking papers, making phone calls to parents or vendors, previewing videos, securing a VCR or other equipment, and using the school's copy machines for producing student materials. So he and the math teacher, like most of their colleagues elsewhere, remain people for whom rollerblades would be in order to meet the day's obligations.

• *Demands from others.* High school teachers are expected to know their subjects inside and out; they are expected to maintain order in their classrooms; they are expected to report instances of abuse and spot signs of behavioral problems; they are expected to be both friendly and demanding of each and every student; and with district and state mandates for students to meet higher academic standards and take tests that can spell the difference between graduating or staying in school longer, teachers are expected to prod students on homework and other assignments and to be personally accountable for how well the students do on tests.

So teaching high school, in addition to knowing one's subject matter thoroughly and being able to convey it to others, requires the grit of a long-distance runner, the stamina of a boxer going 15 rounds, the temperament of a juggler, and the street smarts of a three-card monte dealer.

• *The inherent unreliability of the technology.* Add serious technology use to the mix and a teacher needs infinite patience. Ask even the most dedicated teacher-users about the reliability of these machines and their software. Most schools can't afford on-site technical support. When they do have coordinators and eager students who troubleshoot problems and do the repairs, there are still software glitches and servers that crash, torpedoing lessons again and again. Then new software packages and upgraded ones require more memory and speed from machines that are sorely limited in their capacity. More breakdowns, more pulled hair. These caring and techno-enthusiastic teachers ask, "What did I do to deserve this?"

• *Policymakers' disrespect for teachers' opinions.* Teachers seldom are consulted on which technologies make the most sense for them to use with their students, and what machines and software are both sensible and re-liable for their classrooms. Instead, their classrooms disappear in the equation. Fully stocked labs with donated or purchased equipment appear. Machines pop up on teachers' desks. Administrators exhort teachers to take brand-new courses on technology that the district just made available.

The obvious question that seldom gets asked is this: Why should very busy teachers who are genuinely committed to doing a good job with their students listen to experts' changing advice on technologies when they have to face daily, unyielding working conditions, internal and external demands on their time and stamina, unreliable machines and software, and disrespect for their opinions?

Bashing teachers for not doing more with technology in their classrooms may give us cute media one-liners. What the one-liners miss, however, are the deeper, more consequential reasons for what teachers do every day. What corporate cheerleaders, policymakers, and vendors who have far more access to the media ignore are teachers' voices, the enduring workplace conditions within which teachers teach, inherent flaws in the technologies, and ever-changing advice of their own experts.

Such reasons are ignored because they go to the heart of what happens in schools, are very expensive to remedy, and reflect poorly on corporate know-how in producing machines. Nonetheless, these reasons may have more ex-planatory power for solving the puzzle of extensive home use of computers and limited, low-end classroom use than do the currently fashionable ones.

Larry Cuban is professor emeritus of education at Stanford University and author of numerous books on education, including *The Blackboard and the Bottom Line: Why Schools Can't Be Businesses* (Harvard University Press, 2005). His most recent book is *Cutting Through the Hype: A Taxpayer's Guide to School Reforms* (Education Week Press, 2006), co-authored with Jane L. David.

Seven years later, the opportunities for achieving Edutopia have expanded,
due to the pace of global change and the continuing evolution of the Internet.
Now, in a post-9/11 world, we as Americans can no longer ignore that we live in an
interconnected world. Advances in broadband access, mobile computing, and
educational content on the Internet are making it possible for students to learn in a
24/7/365 world, not limited by a 6/5/180 school calendar. The Internet is the perfect
tool for helping students understand global issues, using e-mail and videoconferencing
to carry out projects with their peers in other countries. The Internet has made learning
"Internet-ional" and carries with it new hope for achieving a more peaceful world.—MC

PUBLISHED MAY 16, 2001

SEEKING EDUTOPIA

[MILTON CHEN]

"My own experience in public school was quite frustrating. I was often bored.
Occasionally, I had a teacher who engaged me, who made me curious and motivated
to learn. I wondered, 'Why can't school be interesting all of the time?'"
—George Lucas

Much of the contemporary education debate can be summarized as proposals
to improve a current system deeply rooted in the distant past. Allen Glenn,
a professor and former dean of education at the University of Washington,
may well be right when he says, "The biggest obstacle to school change is our
memories."

Creating schools for the 21st century requires less time looking in the rearview mirror and more effort anticipating the road ahead. Filmmaker George Lucas, chairman of the educational foundation where I work, is well-known for his prescient view of the transformative effects of technology in the world of entertainment. His work in digital filmmaking is a result of his impulse to, as he puts it, "run down the path more quickly than others and come back and tell them what I've seen." At the foundation that bears his name, our mission is to help educators and the larger public glimpse the future, through a World Wide Web site, films, books, and CDs. Our idealism is unabashedly reflected in the title of our newsletter: *Edutopia*.

The best blueprints for new schools, however, won't emerge from gazing at the blue sky. We only have to set our sights on some courageous pioneers—teachers, principals, and educators at all levels—who are blazing trails to a new horizon. The seeds of the future are being sown in the present, if we only know where to look.

Our vision of the future starts with a story. The setting: a small town in California's central valley. The time: the 1950s. The main character: a young boy, a daydreamer who likes to write stories. He finds most of his schooling irrelevant to his deeper interests. For instance, he asks his mother, "If there is only one God, why are there so many religions?"—a question rich with intellectual possibilities but absent from his grade school textbook.

His one passion: the technology of automobiles. Outside of school, he learns everything he can about cars, from their engines and design to the economics and history of the industry. He fixes cars, races them, and considers a career as a car mechanic. A near-fatal car crash weeks before high school graduation propels him to find a deeper meaning and to pursue further education. After taking courses in writing, philosophy, art, and photography at a nearby junior college, he enrolls in a university with a friend, thinking to continue his photography studies. The photography department turns out to be a film school. He immerses himself in another technology for recording and editing pictures, sound, and music, enabling him to realize his amazing visual imagination.

Many readers can pick up George Lucas's story from there. In 1991, our foundation was born out of his frustration with his own schooling, as well as his faith in the potential of technology to engage many more young learners like himself who learn visually as well as verbally, who like to use their hands as well as their heads, and whose creative and artistic talents go untapped in the textbook-based classroom.

Along our own path, we received wise counsel from our national board of advisers, visionaries in their own right, such as Linda Roberts, the recent director of educational technology for the U.S. Department of Education, and Shirley Malcom, the head of education at the American Association for the Advancement of Science.

During our first few years, we experimented with interactive laserdisc prototypes to demonstrate how advanced technology could revolutionize teaching. But our advisers advised that many promising technologies have foundered on the shoals of school systems unprepared or unwilling to adopt them. Instead, they urged us to find those schools, perhaps only a few in each state, that were quietly innovating and creating a very different kind of future.

They urged us to do what a foundation carrying the name of George Lucas should do: make films about those schools and help the public visualize what our best classrooms and teachers look like. At least then we could point to real schools, real teachers, and real students. Innovation would not be hypothetical. In Immanuel Kant's famous dictum, "the actual proves the possible."

One more thing, they added. It's 1995. There's this thing called the Internet. Schools and teachers are getting connected to it. If it really plays out to provide the educational content of our greatest universities, museums, and libraries, for free, any time, anywhere, it could be the technology to trump all previous technologies in permeating and transforming our schools.

So, we set out to find those unsung heroes. One of our earliest discoveries, in 1996, was a fourth and fifth grade classroom taught by Jim Dieckmann at the Clear View Charter School in Chula Vista, California, not far from the Mexican border. For our first documentary, we filmed his students collecting insect specimens, working in teams to obtain information on their insects from the Web, creating multimedia reports, and with their teacher, developing an assessment rubric to evaluate their use of text, images, graphics, and sound.

The students were connected through a fiber-optic cable connection to San Diego State University, where, through full two-way audio and video, entomologists guided them in examining their insect specimens under an electron microscope. The students' excitement as they prepared to go online with the scientists was palpable. While many fourth graders can barely spell *electron microscope,* let alone use one, this experience magnified for us how the traditional curriculum underestimates the speed and depth of learning done by self-motivated students.

Five years later, that classroom still stands as a model. Skeptics, however, deemed it merely a "stand alone" model, too high-tech and unique. They lamented that their own schools lacked high-speed cable connections and nearby universities with scientists and electron microscopes. Two years ago, the University of Illinois's Beckman Institute for Advanced Science and Technology launched a National Science Foundation–funded program, Bugscope (bugscope.beckman.uiuc.edu), in which students around the country, kindergarten through high school, capture insect specimens, send them to the university, and then schedule the university's electron microscope for an hour. Using their classroom computer and a Web browser, they remotely control the microscope, discussing their insects with the university's entomologists. Bugscope and other projects like it are fulfilling the Internet's promise of breaking down barriers to scientific experts and their high-tech tools.

Technology not only can provide new forms of content and connectivity, but also can transform human roles and relationships in educational systems—perhaps an even greater challenge. Bruce Alberts, president of the National Academy of Sciences, has found that in matters of school reform, human inertia may be stronger than inertia in the physical world. "There is much more inertia in human society than there is in physics," he says. "In physics, if you push on something enough, no matter how heavy, it moves a little bit. Time after time, talented and idealistic people try to improve our schools, instituting major projects with major effort; yet, when the projects end, the schools slide back to where they were before."

Consider, for example, how the Web is changing the balance of power between patients and their physicians, equipping patients with better information to discuss their diagnoses. Technology is also leading schools to recast traditional roles: teachers become learners, and students can become, in a new sense, "student teachers."

In our film, Jim Dieckmann was portraying the new role of "the teacher-learner." No longer the "sage on the stage," but not merely a "guide on the side," Dieckmann was still center stage. He was the hub of his students' learning and the conductor of a symphony of learning resources, including books, the Internet, and other adult experts. He brought the larger world to his students, which in turn expanded his own knowledge of the subject.

Likewise, his students were also taking on new identities as more active, independent learners, assuming greater responsibility for their own learning, as well as the learning of their team members and classmates. As peer tutors and reviewers, they were helping teach one another.

In most schools, students have remarkably little voice in what they are asked to learn and how they learn it. This near-conspiracy to exclude students from a role in instructional decisions extends to the hundreds of educational conferences held each year, which rarely invite students to present their work or discuss their school experiences. While much has been said about the heavy burden of teachers faced with large class sizes, we rarely turn to an overlooked teaching resource already in our classrooms: the students themselves. Students can serve remarkably well as tutors for younger students, peer reviewers for their classmates, and "technology resource specialists" for their teachers.

"Help Wanted: Technologically literate person to create PowerPoint presentations from teachers' lecture notes. Ability to find best Web sites for specific topics, such as the Civil War or animal behavior. Funds limited. Willingness to volunteer appreciated." This want ad describes positions needed in every school across the country. Generation Why, begun in Olympia, Washington, trains students in grades 3-12 to be the perfect solution for overworked teachers needing to learn new technology skills. Now recognized as an exemplary technology project by the U.S. Department of Education, Generation Why has grown to more than 500 schools by placing students into a role formerly confined to graduate students in universities: the teaching assistant.

Unlike some graduate teaching assistants, however, Generation Why students first take a semester course on teaching, learning how to support teachers and effectively integrate technology into the classroom. The program's graduates often go on to serve on school technology and curriculum committees, keep computer labs open after hours, and help train pre-service teachers. They are living examples of the belief, rarely practiced among students, that "the best way to learn something is to teach it."

The ThinkQuest competition for student-designed Web sites (thinkquest.org) carries student work to its fullest realization. The award-winning sites, ranging from the history and appreciation of music, complete with a virtual concert hall, to a comprehensive review of global energy issues, are astonishing in their professional quality, depth of content, and beauty of design. Their sites reveal the most revolutionary role yet: students as designers of curriculum.

As students operate in these new arrangements with each other and with adults, they will need well-developed social and emotional skills. These skills will stand them in good stead as they prepare for the digital workplace, whose job descriptions are constantly evolving and require "just-in-time learning." Daniel Goleman's recent book, *Working with Emotional Intelligence,* describes how successful workplaces, including high-tech firms, organize employees in teams and place a premium on their ability to communicate and manage relationships.

Our best schools are emphasizing this undervalued part of the "invisible curriculum." New York City's Public School 15 in Brooklyn uses the Resolving Conflict Creatively Program developed by the school system and Educators for Social Responsibility. We observed two fifth grade girls role-playing an argument when one of them was not invited to the other's birthday party. One girl calls the other a "lousy" friend: "I have you over to my house all the time, and you couldn't even invite me to your stupid party?" In a second version of the same encounter, she learns to use "I-messages" in expressing her feelings: "I felt hurt and angry when you didn't invite me, because I thought we were good friends." Her friend responds, "My mother told me I could only invite two friends because my cousins were coming. I hope we can keep on being friends."

Such programs reveal a well-kept secret. Emotionally intelligent students perform better on tests and other measures of learning, because they are more equipped to concentrate, persist, and think independently. Common sense and the recent wave of school shootings tell us that schooling must embrace students' hearts as well as their minds, that "high tech" must be accompanied by "high touch." Only teachers, counselors, and administrators can provide the human nurturing and mentoring needed for students to develop their social and emotional skills. No machine ever will.

This new decade presents opportunities to redesign not only human relationships within schools but also the very brick and mortar that surround them. Schools have become remarkably isolated from the rest of society, in physical as well as human terms. As Lee Shulman, president of the Carnegie Foundation for the Advancement of Teaching, has observed, "Teaching has been an activity undertaken behind closed doors between moderately consenting participants."

The coming wave of school construction presents a historic opportunity to rethink the buildings we call schools, in architectural design, physical location, and virtual connections. Some schools are modeling a new paradigm, morphing into more broadly based "community-learning centers" and using their facilities in partnership with colleges, science centers, and community organizations.

At the School of Environmental Studies outside of Minneapolis, the border between school and community has vanished. At the "Zoo School," as it is popularly known, high schoolers attend classes at—the zoo! With access to 2,700 animal species and 500 acres of wetlands and woods, students work alongside the zoo's staff, studying, for instance, the zoo's endangered species, such as the Komodo dragon or trumpeter swan, and accessing professional tools, such as a database on Siberian-tiger genetics. Instead of the game of musical desks played by most high school students every 45 minutes, these students return from their field work to their own cubicles and workstations, arrayed around a central open space used for lectures and group activities. There are now 10 similar "zoo schools" around the country.

For these innovations to spread further, educators and parents, as well as business and community leaders, must first see them and understand them. The public is well known for its attention deficit when it comes to education, but its needs as a visual learner have been largely unmet. Technology itself can help visualize these innovations. We are encouraged by the growing number of our colleagues in school reform groups and foundations who are using video and the Web to share the images, voices, and work of our most inspiring teachers and students.

In working toward greater public understanding of education, we do have one small request. On the front of our staff T-shirt is the word *JARGON* inside a big red circle with a slash through it. The walls erected by "educationese" are high and obstruct the view of many noneducators. One example, "Constructivist pedagogy" should be replaced by "teaching for deep understanding."

Recently I met some middle school students who carry laptops in their backpacks. One boy told me how technology should be not a machine you go *to* but a machine that goes *with you*. He said, somewhat impatiently, "It's a part of my brain. Why would I want to leave it behind in a computer lab?" These students are young explorers in this brave new world of technology. But they might be considered middle-aged.

Even younger students are standing in tidal marshes and at intersections, using palm-size devices to collect and analyze weather and traffic data. Portable computing is already opening up new possibilities for students to learn in and outside of classrooms, nights, weekends, and summers. And then there's this thing called Internet 2.

These developments will continue to force our human institutions of schools to respond. They will raise the most fundamental questions of educational identity and demand more thoughtful answers: What does it mean to be a teacher? How do we define a student? And how should we design our schools?

Our best schools are already providing answers to these questions and demonstrating that our students, not our computers, are the most marvelous learning machines. Children are born wired to learn. Their brighter future is now, right in front of us, if we can only grasp it.

Milton Chen is executive director of the George Lucas Educational Foundation (http://www.glef.org). Previously Chen was founding director of the KQED Center for Education & Lifelong Learning (PBS) in San Francisco. He has also been director of research at the Children's Television Workshop in New York and assistant professor at the Harvard Graduate School of Education.

In our September 2004 Commentary piece we explained that the percentages of the American work force engaged in repetitive manufacturing and administrative support tasks—work relatively easy to computerize—declined dramatically between 1969 and 1999. An update of these trends shows equally startling results. Between May 2000 and May 2006, total employment in the U.S. increased by 7.4 million. Over the same years, the number of workers in manufacturing and administrative support occupations declined by 3.6 million. The figures underscore that the work that provided middle-class wages 50 years ago for many high-school-educated workers will not do so in the years ahead.—FL and RJM

PUBLISHED SEPTEMBER 1, 2004

PREPARING STUDENTS FOR WORK IN A COMPUTER-FILLED ECONOMY

[FRANK LEVY & RICHARD J. MURNANE]

More than half of all American workers use a computer at work, and the percentage is growing rapidly. How should American schools prepare students to thrive in workplaces filled with computers? The answer begins with understanding the work that computers can and cannot do well, so that students can be prepared for work that computers will not be doing.

Start by taking a broad look at the workplace tasks people do in any economy. Every job requires the processing of information. Whether it's words on a page, numbers in a report, the look on a customer's face, the taste of a sauce, the sound of a stumbling automobile engine—people in their daily work process all this information as they decide what to do next. Computers excel at carrying out those information-processing tasks that can be defined in terms of a sequence of rules. Filing and bookkeeping and repetitive manufacturing work are prototypical examples, but others now include issuing airport boarding passes and evaluating mortgage applications. Rules-based tasks are not only the easiest to computerize; they are also the easiest to send offshore to lower-wage countries. In the case of an Indian call center, the "rules" take the form of a step-by-step script that provides responses to most customer questions. As a result of computerization and outsourcing, work for a growing percentage of Americans consists of tasks in which information cannot be processed simply by following rules.

There are three types of workplace tasks that cannot be carried out by following a sequence of rules. The first is identifying and solving new problems—if the problem is new, there are no rules for solving it. We call this kind of problem solving *expert thinking*. A second set of tasks consists of complex human interactions, including leading, teaching, marketing, and negotiating. These tasks cannot be accomplished effectively by following rules because they involve processing vast amounts of information, only some of which is verbal and much of which may be unanticipated when the interaction starts. We call this interactive ability *complex communication*. A third type of workplace task that cannot be described in rules is a set of "simple" physical activities that figure prominently in service-sector jobs like janitorial work, waiting on tables, and security-guard patrols. From a computer's perspective, these jobs are not simple at all, something we can appreciate when we think about what the eye and brain must do to process light hitting the retina into three-dimensional models of the world.

As computers replace humans in rules-based tasks, both directly and by facilitating outsourcing, they have helped dramatically alter the U.S. occupational distribution. The job categories that have grown in importance between 1969 and 1999 are at the two ends of the wage distribution. On the low-wage end, there has been growth in the number of service-sector jobs that almost all humans can do but that are very difficult to program computers to do. At the high-wage end, there has been growth in the numbers of sales, technical, professional, and managerial jobs—jobs that computers do not do well but that well-educated humans do.

The job categories that have declined in importance are administrative-support work and blue-collar work—principally production jobs—that are in the lower middle of the wage distribution. These are the job categories that, historically, provided work for American high school graduates who did not go to college. In this evolving occupational distribution, those students who leave high school with the skills to succeed in the college programs needed to gain access to technical, managerial, and professional jobs will do fine. Those who leave high school without these skills will find themselves competing for the low-wage service jobs.

How can schools prepare students to gain access to and thrive in the growing number of technical and professional jobs? The key is increasing students' ability to engage in expert thinking and complex communication, the two terms we defined above. We do not see expert thinking and complex communication as new subjects to add to the curriculum. Instead, they should be central to the pedagogy for teaching the traditional subjects, all of which retain their importance.

Reading and mathematics are the tools by which students acquire knowledge, and knowledge is critical to expert thinking in any subject domain. Writing is important because it is a key element of complex communication. Science and social studies are at least as important to work and life in a pluralistic democracy as they ever were. What is of growing importance is that instruction in all these core subjects emphasizes identifying and solving problems and the listening, speaking, and writing skills that are central to effective communication.

You will note that we have not mentioned computer skills. In the computerized workplace, a basic understanding of computers is required for most jobs. Providing all students with basic computer skills is a challenge that has been largely met—if facility with computers is defined narrowly.

A 1999 National Research Council report, *Being Fluent with Information Technology,* provides a list of "information-technology skills" that includes using basic operating-system features, using a word processor to create a text document, using the Internet to find information and resources, and using a computer to communicate with others. While a "digital divide" existed 15 years ago between students with these skills and those who lacked them, the increasing availability of computers in schools, homes, and libraries has to a large extent eliminated that divide.

Today's digital divide occurs at a higher level—between students who can use a computer to do valuable work and those who cannot. The same National Research Council report on information technology includes a second list, labeled *intellectual capabilities*. Items on this list include engaging in sustained reasoning, managing complexity, testing solutions, evaluating information, collaborating, and communicating to other audiences.

We see this second list as strikingly similar to the elements of expert thinking and complex communication, capabilities that will determine whether students gain access to the growing number of well-paid jobs or are relegated to the relatively low-paying jobs in the service sector. For this reason, the focus in schools should be on using computers as tools in working on problem solving and complex communication tasks that are at the center of instruction in the core school subjects.

As the country starts a new school year, it is a good time to consider whether our schools are preparing students to thrive in a society full of computers. Two students' responses to a teacher's questions about a historical event illustrate the challenge. This example is taken from a 2001 report from the National Research Council, *Knowing What Students Know: The Science and Design of Educational Assessment*:

STUDENT NO. 1

Q. What was the date of the battle of the Spanish Armada?

A. 1588.

Q. How do you know this?

A. It was one of the dates I memorized for the exam.

Q. Why is the event important?

A. I don't know.

STUDENT NO. 2

Q. What was the date of the battle of the Spanish Armada?

A. It must have been around 1590.

Q. How do you know this?

A. I know the English began to settle in Virginia just after 1600, although I'm not sure of the exact date. They wouldn't have dared start overseas explorations if Spain still had control of the seas. It would have taken a little while to get expeditions organized, so England must have gained naval supremacy somewhere in the late 1500s.

Q. Why is the event important?

A. It marks a turning point in the relative importance of England and Spain as European powers and colonizers of the New World.

Only instruction that prepares students to give the second type of answers will prove valuable in a society filled with computers. So it is appropriate to ask in every subject, Is this the kind of instruction we are providing?

Frank Levy and Richard J. Murnane, both economists, are, respectively, Daniel Rose Professor of Urban Economics at the Massachusetts Institute of Technology and Thompson Professor of Education and Society at Harvard University, both in Cambridge, Massachusetts. This essay is based on their book *The New Division of Labor: How Computers Are Creating the Next Job Market* (Princeton University Press and Russell Sage Foundation, 2004).

PART SIX

DEMOCRACY AND VIRTUE

Nearly a century ago, English judge John Fletcher Moulton identified integrity
with "the settled disposition to do what is right when there is no one to make you
do it but yourself." I have found this description of integrity to be instructive to high
school and college students, as well as to adults in the professions, business, and public
service. The habits of justice, temperance, and courage woven into this disposition,
when they become second nature to us, sustain integrity in public and private.
The best teachers I have known embody these ideals in their way of life.—EJD

PUBLISHED SEPTEMBER 5, 1990

TEACHING INTEGRITY

The Boundaries of Moral Education

[EDWIN J. DELATTRE]

A recent *Wall Street Journal* article on education bore the headline, "School-
teachers Say It's Wrongheaded to Try to Teach Students What's Right." This
view is not new. Four years ago, *Newsweek* magazine described "morals
education" as "a minefield" and asked "whose values" are to be taught.

Teachers and administrators who object to moral education express fear
of stirring unwanted controversy within diverse student populations and
families. Some refuse, as a matter of principle, to teach values—on the
grounds that moral education destroys separation of church and state.
Others insist that "it would be dangerous, sad, and boring to have one
view of morality imposed on our people."

No one familiar with programs that have been foisted upon schools, teachers, and students under the banner of *values* or *moral* education can be entirely unsympathetic to these fears and concerns.

Some programs, such as *values clarification,* are based on a mindless reduction of morality to a matter of personal and arbitrary taste. Students are taught that whether you like genocide or bigotry is roughly the same as whether you like broccoli. Schools are clearly better off avoiding such dangerous folly, especially because these programs teach students nothing about the real nature of principled judgment and conduct.

Other programs are impositional, in the sense that they make pronouncements about morality that are ill-informed, dogmatic, and highly questionable. I have heard students told that there are clear litmus tests for identifying decent people—including where they stand on the rightness of abortion, of homosexuality, or of specific U.S. foreign policies.

Such pronouncements thwart students' learning the undeniable fact that decent and conscientious people can disagree about complex questions of conduct and policy. They are therefore an affront to intellectual honesty and do not belong in schools. Programs with this tone mislead in another way: students deserve to learn that no matter what views individuals hold on complex questions, they may still be deplorable people in their habits of daily life and therefore unworthy of respect and admiration. After all, a person who betrays the trust of others through insider trading is contemptible no matter where he or she stands on abortion.

What this array of harmful and benighted programs shows is that moral education can be and frequently has been done badly. But since virtually everyone knew that already, this was never one of the fundamental questions about moral education.

The fundamental questions for centuries have been these:

What is morality?

Can morality be taught?

Can morality be learned?

Can adults possibly avoid influencing the moral habits and attitudes of the children and youths who keep company with them?

Despite popular prejudices and confusions, these are not unanswerable questions. Broadly put, morality is the achievement of good character and of the aspiration to be the best person you can be. But what is good character and what kind of person should one aspire to become?

The answers are that a good person is one who has integrity and that all of us should aspire to achieve integrity as fully as we can. Literally, integrity means wholeness—being one person in public and private, living in faithfulness to one set of principles whether or not anyone is watching. Integrity is to a person as homogenization is to milk—a single consistency throughout.

But this answer remains too general, because a person can, unfortunately, have bad character in both public and private; a person can be rotten in dealing with strangers and family alike. So, what kind of wholeness is genuine integrity and thus worthy of respect and emulation?

First, integrity is the habit of treating other people fairly—giving them equal initial consideration—just because they are people, and without regard to race or ethnicity or gender. The habit of recognizing other people as important in themselves—and not as objects to be used merely for our own gratification—is called *justice*. It means being able to see things from inside the skin of other people, and no one can do that who hates others because of their skin. It also means making decisions from the principle that everyone deserves to be treated fairly by our daily conduct. Where the habit of justice becomes second nature, it inspires the habit of compassion—the habit of real sensitivity to the pain or suffering of others.

Second, it is the habit of controlling ourselves amid promises of pleasure, and of confining ourselves to healthful pleasures that are not selfishly sought at the expense of others. This habit is called *temperance*.

Third, it is the habit of controlling ourselves amid threats of pain or loss—facing up to clear duties even when doing so risks adverse peer pressure or loss of some other kind. This is the habit of *courage,* and it must be distinguished from cowardice and also from the recklessness to which the young are frequently inclined.

Fourth, it is the habit of gathering evidence conscientiously and relying on it in reaching conclusions and decisions, and the habit of not using deception to manipulate other people for ulterior purposes. These are the habits of *intellectual and moral honesty.*

Now, suppose a person achieves such habits, achieves a substantial degree of integrity. Where will that person stand on abortion? Is it right? Is it wrong? Should it be illegal? Where will the person stand on affirmative action—on the ascription of rights to individuals and of rights to groups?

We cannot know where the person will stand. We can know only that the person will take such questions seriously and seek to answer them conscientiously and with rigorous, logical reasoning and deliberation. We can know that the person will extend humility toward others who are likewise decent enough to be serious. We can know that a person of integrity will understand that morality is above all a matter of taking life and its conduct seriously and will feel kinship toward others who show such seriousness in their lives. This students should have the chance to witness and to grasp.

Can morality be taught? Can it be learned? Since achieving integrity or character excellence is a matter of forming habits, and since both good and bad habits can be formed only by repeating actions over and over again, morality cannot be taught. But because people can become habituated by repeated behavior under responsible and loving training and supervision, the habits of morality can be learned.

Moreover, it is only when such habits have been learned, when the habit of giving consideration to other people has become second nature, that anyone can recognize moral problems, issues, and dilemmas as problems worthy of attention and reflection. For a person who has achieved no habits of justice or temperance or courage, questions of whether to take unfair advantage of others, where to stand on abortion, whether to use illegal drugs, whether to go along with the prevailing fashions of peer pressure, and so on are not questions at all. At most, conversation about them will be only a word game—perhaps a contest to see who can be most clever—insubstantial and without meaning or consequence.

It is for this reason that putative moral education consisting of classroom discussion of controversial issues and putative dilemmas begs all questions of moral decency and moral motivation. Real moral deliberation presupposes learning habits of integrity; what can be taught are the principles of intellectual rigor and reliable thought as they are applied to questions of all kinds—

in philosophy, the sciences, history, literature, theology, and all the other disciplines of inquiry and discovery. This surely, no administrator, teacher, or school worthy of the name would ever seek to evade. Neither would any responsible educator shirk teaching that respect for pluralism and disagreement does not embrace mindless tolerance of behavior and attitudes that are transparently unjust (such as racist supremacism of every kind) or selfishly intemperate (such as violent criminality against others) or manipulatively dishonest (such as cover-ups of corruption), and so on.

Finally, is it possible for adults to be value neutral, to avoid all influence in the formation of the moral and intellectual habits and attitudes of the young? The answer is obviously no. As the great classicist and teacher Gilbert Highet put the point, "[I]t is impossible to have children without teaching them. Beat them, coddle them, ignore them, force-feed them, shun them or worry about them, love them or hate them, you are still teaching them something, all the time."

Most teachers know that they teach about right and wrong by the way they behave. Teachers who behave as if they were value neutral in the presence of the young succeed only in teaching their students that they are being deceptive, probably manipulative. Some students will infer, perhaps unjustly, that their teachers are both liars and cowards. And the more astute students will soon see that attempting to convey value neutrality as an appropriate way to believe and behave condemns life to triviality and education to insignificance, thereby becoming as thoroughly impositional as any other uncritical dogmatism.

It is, after all, possible to train and habituate the young with respect, generosity of spirit, and intellectual honesty. It is possible to help the young learn habits of integrity without "imposition," and it is possible to teach them and help them learn to think with real acumen and rigor.

If their teachers, who are supposed to care about them, and their parents, who are supposed to love them, do not take life that seriously, then the young will learn their habits from the streets, from demagogues, and from entertainment and commercial media that neither care about them nor love them. That is a consequence no adult of integrity can be willing to tolerate.

Edwin J. Delattre is author of *Character and Cops: Ethics in Policing,* now in its fifth edition (American Enterprise Institute Press, 1996), and associate scholar at the American Enterprise Institute. He is professor of philosophy emeritus in the College of Arts and Sciences at Boston University, dean emeritus of the Boston University School of Education, and president emeritus of St. John's College in Annapolis, Maryland, and Santa Fe, New Mexico.

Since this article originally appeared, we've unfortunately experienced other
kinds of national and worldwide crises, such as September 11, the Columbine
shooting, and the Katrina disaster, and there surely will be more tragedies ahead.
Yet children's needs remain the same. Fred Rogers often reminded us that while
the outsides of children's lives have changed over the years, their insides haven't
changed. No matter what the crisis is, children need to feel secure that adults are
doing all they can to keep them safe, they need help dealing constructively with their
own anger, and they need to know they are loved, in good times and in bad.—HBS

PUBLISHED FEBRUARY 27, 1991

HELPING CHILDREN WITH SCARY NEWS

Written in 1991 in Response to the Persian Gulf War

[**FRED ROGERS WITH
HEDDA BLUESTONE SHARAPAN**]

It is certainly understandable that parents, teachers, and caregivers are
struggling with feelings about how to communicate with children about the
current world crisis. War is an emotional issue for all of us. Anything with

This Commentary was initially published under the headline "Notes to Adults on Children's
Concerns About War." The editors agreed to change the title of the piece to "Helping Children
with Scary News—Written in 1991 in Response to the Persian Gulf War" at Sharapan's request.

such potential for loss and devastation is bound to reawaken any previous fears of significant losses in our own lives. We hear news of war with our ears of today and our hearts of the past. Some adults have even told us they are having trouble sorting out their own needs from those of the children.

As with all concerns about childhood, there aren't magic answers. We are glad to share with you some of our reflections about the Persian Gulf crisis, and we hope these thoughts may be helpful for you as you continue to find your own ways of meeting the needs of the children you love and care for. We also hope you realize that you're giving important care to your children just by your wanting to be helpful to them.

ASSURANCE THAT ADULTS WILL TAKE CARE OF THEM. In any fearful time, children need to know they will be safe and that the adults will take care of their needs. Young children are by nature self-centered. If they weren't they wouldn't survive. Naturally they need to be able to trust that their needs will be met. We must protect our children as much as we can, even from our own adult anxieties.

One director of a day-care center told us she could feel comfortable saying to the children, "I'm sad about the war and I'm worried, but I love you and I am here for you." We each have our own ways to say those kinds of messages to children, and sometimes that's even through just our hugs and our warmth.

We can also offer our assurance through our efforts to keep things as normal as possible. During times of stress and uncertainty, young children need most of all to have constancy and predictability in their lives. Knowing what to expect comforts them. Continuity, familiar routines, and traditions can go a long way in providing security and can serve as anchors for families and schools.

LIMITING OUR OWN TELEVISION VIEWING. It's very tempting to get drawn into watching and listening to war news all day and all night, but healthy adults can and must resist that temptation because it can lead to a feeling of helplessness and despair. There isn't anything that casual war observers can do to help make a difference in the Persian Gulf, but there's a lot we can do right in our own homes.

One is to limit the time we devote to television and radio and invest it in being with our children. They can use our attention far better than all the newscasters in the world put together. And as we do something with our children (and grandchildren), the feeling of helplessness about the war can give way to a sense of hope that our children can grow to be adults who will resist the temptation of abusing others.

> **HOW MUCH DO WE TELL THE CHILDREN?** Even if we wanted to, it would be impossible to help young children understand war. It's too horrible. It's too frightening. If they ask any questions at all, they might ask, "What is a war?" and "Are you going to be in it?" Sometimes answering a question with another question gives us a better idea about what a child is concerned about.

"What is a war?" "What do you think a war is?" Each child will then respond from whatever his or her life experience may be. If it's "I don't know," then the simplest reply is best. For example, "War is a very sad, unpleasant thing, and it's not your fault. Children may fight and they may pretend about war, but children don't make real wars, and I hope when you grow up you'll never have to make one either."

Even though young children should be protected against seeing scary images or hearing graphic details on radio or television, older children are probably aware that something serious is happening in the world. They may have heard about the war from other children. Maybe, even more important, they've sensed that the people they love the most—their parents and caregivers—are worried and anxious. If parents don't bring up the subject of the war to them, they may be left at the mercy of their misinterpretations. We heard about one child who was frightened that the bombs would fall on her father's office. It helped her when her parents asked if she knew about the war and let her voice her fears so they could help her know the war is happening far away.

Some children will, because of their own personal fears, need to deny the gravity of such a thing as war. If a child chooses "not to think about it," we must respect that decision. Years later, that child, grown older, will be better equipped to deal with harsh reality.

BEING GOOD LISTENERS. One of the best ways grown-ups help children is by being empathetic listeners. We have long believed that whatever is mentionable can be more manageable. If we want to encourage our children to share their concerns with us, then our questions can be more important than answers. The way we help our children "talk" is by showing the interest we have in what's important to them.

Parents may want to ask their school-age children if they know why the news is on television so much, or if they know what the people on television are talking about. One mother told us she asked her five-year-old if he knew what was on the news, and she was surprised when he told her that "a man went into another 'city' and took it over . . . he was told to get out and he didn't . . . so we made a war to make him get out." She was stunned that he knew about the situation in such clear terms. She hadn't mentioned it up to that time, thinking it would be better to wait until he brought it up. Where had he heard about it? "From the kids on the school bus," he told her. Her question gave both the mother and son a good springboard for their discussion, and it also gave them a stronger foundation for continued talks in future years for whatever may be important to share.

Listening doesn't happen only through our ears. Children have many ways to let us know that something upsets them. People who are close to children can trust their instincts to know when their children need reassurance and help from them, and they can also trust that their children have ways to let them know when they've heard enough.

When we can be open to whatever our children tell us, we will probably find that the current news of world stress has triggered some other worries they've had at home or at school, so families may be able to benefit in many ways from these discussions.

CONCERNS ABOUT CHILDREN'S WAR PLAY. Playing about war is very different from having a real war. Play is one of the important ways children can work through their concerns. Of course war play can become scary or unsafe, and at times like that children need to know adults are nearby to help reassure them, to stop the play when it becomes too scary, and to redirect the play into caring and nurturing themes, perhaps by suggesting the building of a hospital for the wounded people, or tents and homes where the soldiers could go to eat and sleep.

HELPING CHILDREN DEAL WITH THEIR EVERYDAY CONFLICTS. Maybe most important of all is helping our children find peaceful resolution to their everyday conflicts. Anger is a natural and normal feeling, in families and among friends. Besides allowing children the right to their anger, we can also help them find healthy things to do with their angry feelings—things that don't hurt others or themselves or damage things. We adults can help them think about creative and constructive solutions to their conflicts. If we can help children deal with their angry feelings in healthy ways, we are giving them useful tools that will serve them all life long, and helping them to be the world's future peacemakers.

Fred Rogers died in 2003. The company he founded, Family Communications, Inc., continues the work that carries on his legacy. Rogers is best known for *Mister Rogers' Neighborhood,* the long-running children's television show he launched in 1966. The show was made available for national distribution in 1968. In 2002, Rogers received the Presidential Medal of Freedom, the nation's highest civilian honor.

Hedda Bluestone Sharapan currently serves as director of Early Childhood Initiatives for Family Communications. She worked with Fred Rogers for 38 years and has conducted numerous workshops for early-childhood professionals and parents on topics including helping children deal with anger and seeing the world through the eyes of a child.

Involving all students during their later elementary and secondary school education in practical civics experience so as to develop both their citizen skills and the desire to use them, under the rule of law, can enrich schools, students, and communities alike. Where teachers have made such efforts, the children have responded responsibly and excitedly to the frequent surprise and respect of their elders. Schooling for informed and experienced participation in democratic processes is a major reservoir of future democracy and a profound human resource to be nurtured.—Ralph Nader, February 1, 1992, in *The Concord Principles: An Agenda for a New Initiatory Democracy*

PUBLISHED APRIL 7, 1993

TEACHING THE "OTHER HALF" OF DEMOCRACY'S STORY

[RALPH NADER]

In response to signs in our society that citizen participation in our democracy continues to lag, particularly among young people, many in the education community have called for more attention to civic education in our schools. Yet civics as a course of instruction seems to invite more than its share of collective yawns inside and outside the classroom. What is needed is not more of the same old civics but a different type of civics—one that is rooted in the community, in solving problems, and in learning citizen skills.

Our schools do not teach chemistry without a laboratory, cooking without a kitchen, or computer programming without computers. Likewise, civics cannot be properly taught without using the community as a natural laboratory so that students can learn by doing, by connecting with problem definition and response where they live.

Generations of U.S. students have viewed civics as a dull, abstract, and unmemorable subject. This is so in part because instruction materials have been shorn of the grist of civic history—the controversy, struggles over injustice between parties, and interests having proper names, brand names, and heroic names.

Rarely do these books offer students a real stake in their society, with an opportunity to use their skill to overcome apathy, ignorance, greed, or abuses of power. Rarely do U.S. history textbooks offer students materials about citizen struggles to make this country more democratic and free. From minorities of one to mass movements, Americans repeatedly have rescued their country from shame, error, cruelty, and decline. The neglect of textbooks in not deeply reflecting this democratic tradition has been costly to both the quality of our democracy and the quality of our educational institutions.

Furthermore, most civics textbooks continue to define *good citizenship* in a rote fashion, as obeying the law, paying taxes, voting, and when called upon, serving in the military and on jury duty. A 1989 People For the American Way survey found that young people today "have absorbed only half of democracy's story, perceiving the virtue of our system of government only in the rights and freedoms it provides, not in the accompanying responsibilities it bestows." When asked to describe a "good citizen," students responded that "the task of being a good citizen carries no additional meaning or special responsibility beyond simply being a 'good person.'" The basic civic duty to vote was mentioned by only 12 percent of the respondents as a component of citizenship.

Yet the People For the American Way survey also found an eagerness among young people to become connected to the world. Of the students surveyed, 51 percent favored making community service a requirement for high school graduation, and 89 percent agreed that volunteer service work should be rewarded with school credit.

Students need environments that spawn maturity and creativity on their part by participating in building democracy throughout the community. Too much commercial entertainment, MTV, videos, and other corporate upbringings absorb their lives and detach them from adults and hands-on civic experience. As the Carnegie Foundation for the Advancement of Teaching's 1987 report on student service concluded, "Teenagers in America grow up in the shadows of adult life," unconnected to the larger world.

Learning good citizenship needs to become a high priority in our schools, because it combines a requirement of proficiency in basic education with experience. It connects knowledge to its application fueled by the student motivation that proceeds from being taken seriously and given responsibility in association with adults from the community. Bridging the gap between classroom learning and community experience is a way of connecting students to purposeful learning that transcends listlessness and restlessness on the one hand and excessive vocational or trade-school instrumentalism on the other hand.

Numerous educators have tried to remedy the low priority placed on civic education. But until teachers are free to teach students how to question authority and challenge the status quo in their community when democracy is obstructed, little will change. We need to change the nature of civic education in the United States toward imbuing our young people with a proud sense of the history of citizen participation, and a sense of the possibility that they too can make the world a better place to live. Students must recognize that citizenship in the United States involves far more than freedoms and liberties. Rights are not enough. Our young people must have the skills and the experience to practice and even pioneer active citizenship. Indeed, there can be no daily democracy without daily citizenship.

It is in this spirit that the Center for Study of Responsive Law and Essential Information has produced *Civics for Democracy: A Journey for Teachers and Students,* written by Katherine Isaac. The book contains four sections: (1) profiles of students in action, with case studies, including high school students in Coral Springs, Florida, who successfully campaigned to save the largest stand of cypress trees in their county from development; (2) a history of five major citizen movements (civil rights, labor, women's rights, consumer, and environmental) that details how citizens throughout U.S. history have produced change; (3) techniques for democratic participation that include the tools citizens have used to strengthen our democracy (from citizen lobbying to initiative and referendum); and (4) 10 projects that students can undertake in their schools (such as an energy-waste hunt) and communities (such as a voter-participation survey).

Civics for Democracy profiles the active lives of citizen-activists Thurgood Marshall, Ella Baker, Malcolm X, Mother Jones, Jeannette Rankin, and Esther Peterson as well as the struggles and accomplishments of the Brotherhood of Sleeping Car Porters, the United Farmworkers, and Greenpeace. Also included in the text are 75 ideas for student activities and an extensive list of resources from citizen groups around the country.

Although many teachers have received *Civics for Democracy* with enthusiasm, they note that principals, school boards, and vested interests in turning high schools into vocational schools for industry can provide powerful obstacles to teaching civics from the classroom to community projects.

Where different conditions prevail, where teachers and principals and school boards have shed their inhibitions to confront realities past and present, students are being given problems to analyze and solutions to ponder and advance in their own neighborhoods, communities, states, nations, or right inside their own schools. Examples of student participation include students in Salt Lake City who successfully lobbied their legislators to clean up toxic waste, and students in Washington who saved their school thousands of dollars in electricity bills by monitoring energy waste.

It is time for schools to make civic training at least as high a priority as sports, music, or computer training. Most civics courses have presented general principles of rights and responsibilities, such as the right to vote or the duty to serve on juries. But they have failed to translate these principles into concrete educating for civic action.

Civic participation is a formula for human happiness—both private and public. It is more than a slogan to be intoned; it is a delight to be savored as an essential quality of life that makes democracy both a daily and an authentic reality. What a shame it is for us not to convey that capability to the next generation of Americans—and the awesome problems they will have to confront civically or suffer supinely. To meet this challenge, teachers, school administrators, curriculum specialists, and professors of education must reassess and fundamentally change the nature of civic education in the United States.

Ralph Nader is a consumer advocate and founder of the Center for Study of Responsive Law. A long-time political advocate, Nader also founded the national nonprofit citizen advocacy group Public Citizen in 1971. He has run for president four times, in 1992, 1996, 2000, and 2004.

I wrote this essay in a state of terror, still shaken by the sights, sounds, and smells of mass murder. I tried to connect what I had experienced with my deepest beliefs about education and the future of our democratic society. One lesson of that awful day, I concluded, was that we are all in this together, this struggle to create a better future. The public schools must stress our common humanity, not divide us by our ancestry. They must cultivate the skills and knowledge to advance our common aspirations and unite us in our duty to the res publica, the public thing, the common good.—DR

PUBLISHED OCTOBER 17, 2001

NOW IS THE TIME TO TEACH DEMOCRACY

[DIANE RAVITCH]

On the morning of September 11, 2001, I was sitting at my kitchen table, enjoying a second cup of coffee and reading the morning paper. A friend called to tell me that a plane had just crashed into the World Trade Center. I live about three blocks from the waterfront in Brooklyn, directly across the river from Lower Manhattan, so I ran to the harbor. Just as I arrived, the second plane crashed into the south tower of the World Trade Center. Along with about six others, I stood there wordless as we watched huge balls of flame and smoke erupting from the two buildings. On that bright blue, cloudless morning, the air in the harbor was filled as far as the eye could see with tiny bits of paper, like confetti in a ticker-tape parade, the paper blown off the desks of people who worked in the upper floors of the burning buildings.

All that day, ashes and soot rained down on my neighborhood. Cars were coated with the airborne ash, and a distinctive sickening smell, something akin to burning plastic, permeated the air.

Thousands of our fellow citizens were killed in the conflagration. They were people of all races, religions, ethnicities, and social origins. Most were Americans, some were not. The hundreds of rescuers who died when the buildings collapsed were trying to save human lives, without distinction to anyone's color, beliefs, or national origin. By day's end, New Yorkers were lining up at emergency centers to give blood or to offer supplies or to volunteer in any way that seemed useful. The outpouring of volunteers was so large that many were turned away. So much for those who have decried the decline of civic participation in the United States.

Since the mass murders, educators have been opining about how we must change what we teach our children. We must teach tolerance, they say, as if our children were somehow responsible for what happened because their teachers had failed to teach them tolerance. Of course we must teach tolerance, but we must not teach children to tolerate those who hijack commercial jetliners and kill innocent victims. We must not teach children to tolerate fanaticism, be it political or religious. (Perhaps we could engage in civic dialogues with educators in the countries that the terrorists came from, to share what we know about teaching tolerance.)

Others have said that the events of September 11 demonstrate the necessity for a multicultural curriculum. Again, the implication is that this unprecedented atrocity was caused by a failure in the schools' curriculum, rather than by heartless, inhumane terrorists. For those who wish to see some responses by educators, I recommend an article in the *Washington Post* by Valerie Strauss on October 1, 2001. Educators quoted in the article claim that the tragedy proves that American schools must now teach more multiculturalism.

I beg to differ. I have long urged that American students need to learn more world history (and American history that includes accurate accounts of the experience of our diverse people). In the late 1980s I helped to draft the California history and social science curriculum, which is the only one in the nation that requires three years of world history. That curriculum includes the study of Western, Islamic, Indian, African, Asian, and Latin American civilizations. Certainly our students need a solid grounding in world history. This kind of knowledge is invaluable for everyone, but I reject the view that the murderous behavior of terrorists was linked in any way to what our students did not know about the terrorists' culture or worldview.

If curriculum reformers agreed on more time for the study of world history, that would be a major improvement in all of our schools. However, what they have in mind is not more world history but more "multiculturalism," more attention to our own racial and ethnic differences. No one addressed this issue more forcefully than the late Albert Shanker, president of the American Federation of Teachers. I was with him in 1995 in Prague when he discussed multiculturalism with educators from Eastern and Western Europe. Shanker warned that multiculturalism, as it is taught in the United States, is dangerous for a democratic, multiethnic society because it encourages people "to think of themselves not as individuals, but primarily in terms of their membership in groups." By focusing on differences instead of commonalities, Shanker said, this kind of education does not increase tolerance; on the contrary, it feeds racial and ethnic tensions and erodes civil society, which requires a sense of the common good, a recognition that we are all members of the human race.

Shanker noted that multicultural education teaches cultural relativism because it implies that "no group may make a judgment on any other." Yet all societies must establish basic values and guidelines for behavior. Now, in the wake of the terrorist attacks, we hear expressions of cultural relativism when avant-garde thinkers tell us that we must try to understand why the terrorists chose to kill thousands of innocent people, and that we must try to understand why others in the world hate America. Perhaps if we understood why they hate us, then we could accept the blame for their actions.

I suggest that we reject this blame-the-victim approach. I suggest that what our schools must do is to teach young people the virtues and blessings of our democratic system of government. Our ability to defend what we hold dear depends on our knowledge and understanding of it. If we value a free society, we must know about its origins and its evolution. If we value our rights and freedoms, we must understand how we got them and what it would mean to live in a society that did not have them. A good place for teachers to begin is with the *National Standards for Civics and Government,* published in 1994 by the Center for Civic Education.

To be sure, our democratic practices are not universal, even though almost all of them were clearly articulated in the Universal Declaration of Human Rights, which was endorsed by the United Nations in 1948. It is true that there are many societies that treat women as beasts of burden. There are societies that do not choose their leaders. There are societies where the government and religious authorities decide who is allowed to speak and write. There are societies where free public education does not exist. There are societies where homosexuals are rounded up and imprisoned. There are societies where our Western legal concepts of due process are unknown.

Some of these societies hate us because they hate our way of life. They think it is decadent. They think we are decadent because we protect freedom of speech, allowing people to read, say, and write whatever they want; because we protect freedom of religion, allowing "truth" and "untruth" to be taught without any regulation; because we grant equal rights to men and women, allowing women to be educated to the same extent as men and to advance in the same professions.

Certainly other generations of Americans understood that these rights and freedoms were part of the American way of life. The "greatest generation" that saved the world from fascism and Nazism knew that they were defending these rights and freedoms. The Cold War generation that helped to bring down Soviet totalitarianism understood the importance of these rights and freedoms.

We do not know what sacrifices will be required of us in the months and years ahead. What we should know is the importance of teaching our children about democracy, freedom, human rights, the principle that every person is equal before the law, and the value of the individual. These are ideas with a long history. Our children need to know them.

Diane Ravitch is an education historian and a former assistant U.S. secretary of education under President George H. W. Bush. She was appointed by the Clinton administration to serve two terms on the National Assessment Governing Board, which supervises the National Assessment of Educational Progress. Now a research professor of education at New York University, she is a senior fellow at both the Brookings Institution, in Washington, D.C., and the Hoover Institution, in Stanford, California.

Since 2002, when my article was originally published, the need of the world for wise leaders has only increased. Numerous foolish leaders, in the United States and abroad, have squandered the human and material resources available to their nations. Some of these leaders—individuals with educations in top-branded schools— have been among the worst offenders. In the United States, enforcement of the No Child Left Behind Act has only exacerbated the situation, transforming schools into mindless test-preparation centers and diverting whatever efforts schools might have made to educate their students to be not only superficially smart but also wise.—RJS

PUBLISHED NOVEMBER 13, 2002

TEACHING FOR WISDOM IN OUR SCHOOLS

[ROBERT J. STERNBERG]

The top-level managers who brought down companies such as Enron, Global Crossing, and WorldCom were, for the most part, nothing if they were not smart and well-educated. Yet one cannot help feeling that something fundamental was missing in the way they were educated. Similarly, today's consummate terrorist defies the stereotype of the poorly educated ignorant peasant who, having nothing better to do, joins up with a movement and blindly follows orders while showing no personal initiative at all. On the contrary, many of the terrorists who are covertly walking our streets are smart and well-educated—in the United States in some cases. When their plans go awry, they use their wits to figure out how to get those plans back on track. Once again it appears that something was fundamentally wrong in their education.

What is that something? I believe it is that, for the most part, we are teaching students to be intelligent and knowledgeable but not how to use their intelligence and their knowledge. Schools need to teach for wisdom, not just for factual recall and superficial levels of analysis.

When schools teach for wisdom, they teach students that it is important not just what you know but how you use what you know—whether you use it for good ends or bad. They are teaching for what the Bush administration referred to recently, in a White House conference, as the "fourth R": responsibility. Smart but foolish and irresponsible people, including, apparently, some who run or have run major businesses in our country, exhibit four characteristic fallacies in their thinking.

The *fallacy of egocentrism* occurs when people think the world centers around them. Other people come to be seen merely as tools in the attainment of their goals, to be used and then discarded as the egomaniacs' needs change. Why would smart people think egocentrically? Conventionally smart people often have been so highly rewarded for being smart that they lose sight of the needs and desires of others.

Wisdom requires one to know what one knows and does not know, as well as what can be known and cannot be known at a given time and place. Smart people often lose sight of what they do not know, leading to the second fallacy.

The *fallacy of omniscience* results from people's starting to feel that not only are they expert in whatever they trained for, but they also are all-knowledgeable about pretty much everything. They then can make disastrous decisions based on knowledge that is incomplete but that they do not recognize as such.

The *fallacy of omnipotence* results from the feeling that if knowledge is power, then omniscience is total power. People who are in positions of power may start to imagine themselves to be all-powerful. Worse, they forget the old saw that power corrupts, but absolute power corrupts absolutely. At the same time, they fail to reckon with the potential consequences of their actions because of the fourth fallacy.

The *fallacy of invulnerability* comes from people's view that if they are all-knowing and all-powerful, they can do what they want. And because they are all-knowing, they can get away with anything. Most likely they convince themselves they won't get caught. Even if they do, they figure they can weasel their way out of being punished because they are smarter than those who have caught up with them.

If foolish (but smart and often highly accomplished) people commit these fallacies, what do wise people do?

I define wisdom as *the application of intelligence and experience toward the attainment of a common good.* This attainment involves a balance among (a) intrapersonal (one's own), (b) interpersonal (other people's), and (c) extrapersonal (more than personal, such as institutional) interests, over the short and long terms. Thus, wise people look out not just for themselves but also for all toward whom they have any responsibility.

An implication of this view is that simply being smart is not enough. It is important to be wise too.

There are several reasons why schools should seriously consider including instruction in wisdom-related skills in the school curriculum.

First, knowledge is insufficient for wisdom and certainly does not guarantee satisfaction, happiness, or behavior that looks beyond self-interest. Wisdom seems a better vehicle to the attainment of these goals.

Second, wisdom provides a way to enter considered and deliberative values into important judgments. One cannot be wise and at the same time impulsive, mindless, or immoral in one's judgments.

Third, wisdom represents an avenue to creating a better, more harmonious world. Dictators such as Adolf Hitler and Joseph Stalin may have been knowledgeable. They may even have been good critical thinkers, at least with regard to the maintenance of their own power. They were not wise.

Fourth and finally, students, who later will become parents and leaders, are always part of a greater community. Hence, they will benefit from learning to judge rightly, soundly, and justly on behalf of their community.

If the future is plagued with conflict and turmoil, this instability does not simply reside *out there somewhere.* It resides and has its origin *in ourselves.* For all these reasons, students need not only to recall facts and to think critically (and even creatively) about the content of the subjects they learn, but also to think wisely about it.

Wisdom can be taught in the context of any subject matter. Our own current research, funded by the W. T. Grant Foundation, involves infusing teaching for wisdom into American history. Students learn to think wisely, and especially to understand things from diverse points of view across time and space. For example, what one group might call a "settler," another might call an "invader." What one group might call "Manifest Destiny," another group might call "land theft." Students also learn that in the current world, peace, or at least absence of conflict, depends in large part on being able to understand how other nations and cultures see problems and their solutions differently from the way we do. The goal is not necessarily to accept these other points of view, or even necessarily to achieve some kind of accommodation, but rather to understand that resolution of difficult life problems requires people to want to understand each other and to reach a resolution, whenever possible, that all of those people can somehow live with. In our own research, students being taught to think wisely are being compared with a control group that learns the historical material in a standard way.

The road to teaching for wisdom is bound to be a rocky one. First, entrenched educational structures, whatever they may be, are difficult to change. Wisdom is not taught in schools. In general, it is not even discussed.

Second, many people will not see the value of teaching something that does not have as its primary focus the raising of conventional test scores. Teaching for wisdom is not inconsistent with raising test scores, but teaching to tests is not its primary goal. Teaching for wisdom relates to President Bush's "fourth R"—responsibility—more closely than it relates to the conventional "three R's" that tend to be tested.

Third, wisdom is much more difficult to develop than is the kind of achievement that can be developed and then readily tested via multiple-choice tests, such as "What is the capital of France?"

Finally, people who have gained influence and power in a society via one means—through money, high test scores, parental influence, or whatever—are unlikely to want either to give up that power or to see a new criterion be established on which they do not rank as favorably. Thus, there is no easy path to wisdom or teaching for wisdom. There never was, and probably never will be.

Wisdom might bring us a world that would seek to better itself and the conditions of all the people in it. At some level, we as a society have a choice. What do we wish to maximize through our schooling? Is it just knowledge? Is it just intelligence? Or is it also wisdom? If it is wisdom, then we need to put our students on a much different course. We need to value not only how they use their outstanding individual abilities to maximize their attainments, but how they use their individual abilities to maximize the attainments of others as well.

We need, in short, to value wisdom. And then we need to remember that wisdom is not just about what we think but, more important, how we act.

Robert J. Sternberg is dean of the School of Arts and Sciences at Tufts University in Medford, Massachusetts. He is author of several books, including *Thinking Styles* (Cambridge University Press, 1997).

PART SEVEN

CHANGE
AND REFORM

The wait for a better alignment of schooling with the people's expectations for it continues. But if a hypothesis that emerged for me during my recent writing of a book entitled *Romances with Schools* (2004) should gain support, we might well anticipate the dawning of a new day. It became quite apparent to me that schooling's fall from grace parallels the markedly increased intervention of federal policies in local schools. Meanwhile, the annual Gallup poll of public opinion continues to reveal steady and increasing satisfaction with the schools attended by the local young. Perhaps the new day we need is part of an old one: educators and lay citizens joined in determining the why, what, and how of the schooling experience.—JIG

PUBLISHED APRIL 23, 2003

A NATION IN WAIT

[JOHN I. GOODLAD]

National commissions have become a common way of addressing problems or setting agendas pertaining to major issues of our time. The National Commission on Excellence in Education was one of these, classified as agenda-setting in a recent study conducted by the Annie E. Casey Foundation. Presumably, an agenda-setting commission sets a clear purpose, proposes necessary new conditions to be put in place or present ones to be strengthened (preferably in specific recommendations), and suggests

The author wishes to thank Janice Nittoli of the Human Services Workforce Initiative of the Annie E. Casey Foundation for her report, especially for the criteria an agenda-setting commission should meet.

strategies for effecting constructive changes that include identifying problems needing to be overcome.

These expectations were laid out in the six-point charge from then–U.S. Secretary of Education Terrel H. Bell. It is short on requesting strategies but does call for defining "problems which must be faced and overcome if we are successfully to pursue the course of excellence in education." Secretary Bell assumed there to be a "widespread public perception that something is seriously remiss in our educational system." Apparently the commission thought it necessary to heat up this perception, as evidenced by the oft-quoted sentence in the second paragraph of its report: "If an unfriendly foreign power had attempted to impose on America the mediocre educational performance that exists today, we might well have viewed it as an act of war."

The opening sentence is crisp: "Our nation is at risk." Of what? Of "our once unchallenged pre-eminence in commerce, industry, science, and technological innovation . . . being overtaken by competitors throughout the world." The frenzy of media attention to the report removed for many people a feeling of needing to read it. Matters of substance quickly lost out to an insatiable media appetite for horror stories of school practices to confirm our state of crisis.

Two professional colleagues—good friends—and I were inescapably caught up in the hurricane of hyped-up attention. The press and nearly every report of the commissions appointed by the new "education" governors cited whatever negative they could find in our respective comprehensive studies published in 1983 and 1984: Ernest L. Boyer's *High School* appearing just before *A Nation at Risk,* and Theodore R. Sizer's *Horace's Compromise* and my *A Place Called School* appearing several months afterward. Callers were little interested in the long-standing problems we had identified or in our recommendations. They sought more bad news.

Five years later, colleagues and I traversed the country in a study of the education of educators, probing into the various involvements of colleges of education, the arts and sciences, and participating schools. We found changes of the kind recommended by the national commission and in assorted earlier reports. Few of the future teachers we interviewed knew of *A Nation at Risk* or, for that matter, that a substantial school reform movement was still being sustained in the policy arena. Most were intensely focused on being prepared to manage a classroom some months later. They were little interested in the larger context of the necessary schooling of the nation's young.

I had some lively discussions with university faculty members, most of whom were familiar with *A Nation at Risk*. The dean of biological sciences in a major university said, passionately, that it had not gone far enough in scaring the people. As a result, the nation's leaders had not risen sufficiently to the commission's call for the necessary crusade to upgrade the quality of our schools.

My take on the impact of the report is different. First, as I have stated above, media overkill turned attention away from its substance. Second, the widespread perception that the commission viewed our schools to be a major factor, if not *the* major factor, in the rise and fall of the economy opened up an avenue of criticism that was much traveled in subsequent years. Third, the militaristic language was, indeed, widely viewed as stimulating a crusade.

Regarding my second point, skepticism about the close connection between schooling and the economy came from many sources, including some economists. Critics have cited a poll taken soon after the report's release and again six or seven years later—a lapse of time not sufficient for graduates of revamped schools to have entered the workforce. In the first poll, Japan's economy received first-place ranking in the world, a condition that those polled said would last for years. In the second poll, Japan was replaced by the United States. Neither the media nor policymakers praised the schools for this remarkable turnaround.

Regarding the third point, no massive commitment of resources followed the commission's report. President Reagan had come into office with the expectation that the federal Department of Education would be eliminated. Advised that the American people were profoundly interested in education and deeply concerned about schooling, he endorsed the report. It was politically wise to do so.

I turn now to my first point about *A Nation at Risk* roiling the waters of concern for our schools but not managing to draw nationwide attention to its recommendations for navigating them. Some of the reasons arose, I believe, out of the national context at the time and the report's intersection—or lack of intersection—with it.

Given its brevity, the report is surprisingly comprehensive. There is something in it for a wide range of potential actors, and many of the recommendations are directed to specific groups. The recommendations were sensible, relevant, doable, and unlikely to provoke controversy. Nearly all had appeared in earlier reports on needed school improvement. Those of the much-respected James B. Conant in particular come to mind: *The American High School Today* (1959), which provided direction nationwide to school boards, and his *The Education of American Teachers* (1963), which made recommendations for teacher education. Surely it is useful to repeat much-needed but little-implemented recommendations of the past. An implicit message of *A Nation at Risk* is that some important school business had been seriously neglected over the years, and those responsible needed to work harder and be held accountable.

There is nothing wrong with such a message. It just did not respond to the report's self-imposed challenge of rectifying educational conditions of such mediocrity that they might well have been regarded as something imposed upon us by an unfriendly foreign power. The scary message simply added to the belief that had been festering for some years—that America's once-vaunted system of public schooling was failing us.

Knocking our schools has often been in fashion. But the targets usually have been specific: the curriculum, progressive methods of teaching, administrators, teachers' unions, schools of education, and so on. This is not the place to go into the history of schooling's fall from grace that became sharply apparent in the late 1960s—not local schools, but our system of public schooling. What Robert M. Hutchins, former president of the University of Chicago, wrote in 1972 presaged the context into which came *A Nation at Risk* in 1983: "But nobody has a kind word for the institution that was only the other day the foundation of our freedom, the guarantee of our future, the cause of our prosperity and power, the bastion of our security, the bright and shining beacon that was the source of our enlightenment, the public school." What the people wanted, at a minimum, was a rekindling of that beacon.

It is incorrect to say that *A Nation at Risk* made no positive impact. We need not look for it in the stream of state reports and politically driven school reform proposals it spawned, even though the report was cited as the justifying icon for most of them. What it did do was stimulate a surge of support from private philanthropy for innovative school improvement initiatives. The need for such was in the air, catching up the interest of school personnel and an impressive array of leaders with ideas. There was not then as there is now a federal mandate siphoning off educators' time and energy and whatever in teaching and the curriculum appears not to contribute directly to higher test scores.

In 1999, the Institute for Educational Inquiry hosted some 1,600 delegates from 21 of these initiatives that were breaking new ground in school renewal. The commitment, energy, and excitement engendered was palpable. Nearly all had received both start-up and subsequent funding from a wide array of foundations. Some of these initiatives have since disappeared, others are suffering from a lack of adequate financial support, and all are in danger of losing out to preparing students for test-taking in the time commitments of participants.

The commission named by Secretary Bell is to be commended for addressing shortcomings in the major factors contributing to academic performance, not just outcomes measured by tests. What the commission appears not to have reckoned on, however, was the continuing public expectation of educational attention to all four of the traditional purposes of schooling in our democracy: the personal, social, and vocational as well as the academic. Two of the comprehensive studies mentioned earlier delved deeply into this issue, concluding independently in chapters so titled that "We Want It All."

One of those studies, sampling 8,624 parents, 1,350 teachers, and 17,163 students, reported the first two of those groups to perceive attention to the academic in their schools to be about right. Students wanted it halved! Parents and students would double attention to the personal. Teachers would triple it! Those and other supporting data were shared with the commission in one of its scheduled public hearings.

There is plenty of evidence to support the observation that public expectations for attention to these four educational goals are as high or higher today. But have we been beguiled into assuming that the academic, assessed by tests, begets understanding and desired behaviors in these other domains? If so, tomorrow's adults and the nation will pay dearly for today's egregious mistake.

While we have been narrowing the scope of academic learning, cognitive psychologists have been telling us that the transfer of learning across contexts is quite limited. To assume that high test scores on school subjects predict such desirable personal and social attributes as civility, decency, civicness, honesty, dependability, compassion, creativity, and even good work habits is folly. For corporate employers to count on test scores predicting the qualities they want in their employees is an exercise in futility.

People who believe that academic learning is the sole purpose of schooling should be aware that even students who do well on tests in school subjects commonly fail to connect what they appear to have mastered to contexts outside of school for which it is relevant. Researchers Stephen Ceci and Antonio Roazzi concluded from available research "that even those students at good universities who take ample science, statistics, and math courses do not transfer the principles they learn . . . to novel contexts." Nationwide implementation of the federal No Child Left Behind Act of 2001 will not give us the schools we need.

The National Commission on Excellence in Education did what it was asked to do. The lesson jumping out at us is that not another commission, not a series of education summits, and not another spate of school reform mandates will set the stage for the renaissance in educating the young that so urgently beckons. We should have assembled 20 years ago a task force with a charge and resources at least comparable to those that launched our exploration of outer space. With a nucleus of full-time members, it would consist of a diverse array of practitioners with track records of school innovation and renewal; researchers distinguished for their work in such fields as cognition, pedagogy, economics, sociology, human development, comparative education, schooling, and more; and creative others who have connected their fields of inquiry to education, particularly the relationship between education and democracy.

The charge to such a task force can be encompassed in one long sentence: Plan the design and development of an educational system aligned with the nation's expectations for it, with the relevant knowledge we have now that we did not have when the present system hardened into place a century ago, and with the 21st-century realities of our transforming world.

It is not too late. But continuing delay places this nation at risk far beyond that feared by the National Commission on Excellence in Education. For how much longer must we wait?

John I. Goodlad is cofounder of the Center for Educational Renewal at the University of Washington in Seattle and president of the Institute for Educational Inquiry, also in Seattle. He is author of numerous books, including *A Place Called School* (McGraw-Hill, 1984) and *Romances with Schools: A Life of Education* (McGraw-Hill, 2004).

Seventeen years later, all six cliches mentioned in my essay remain articles of faith across most of the profession and the population—a sorry testament to the tenacity of conventional wisdom. Time has shot the biggest reality holes through "local control" (consider No Child Left Behind); "politicians should keep away" (they are, in fact, today's lead reformers); and "choice = vouchers" (observe 3,600 charter schools, just for starters). The new cliche in need of challenge is the assumption that "standards-based reform is a slam-dunk." We've seen far too many examples of bad standards, inept tests, and toothless accountability systems.—CEF

PUBLISHED JANUARY 25, 1989

QUESTIONING CLICHES OF EDUCATION REFORM

[CHESTER E. FINN JR.]

American education is awash these days in hoary cliches and trendy maxims thought to be true because they sound so plausible, because we've been hearing them for so long, or because someone we're inclined to trust is uttering them.

But many of these shards of conventional wisdom are unproven. A large number are oversimplifications at best, falsehoods at worst. Some are lightly camouflaged fragments of inertia, self-interest, or wishful thinking.

Yet in these terms the nation's education dilemmas are being framed—and the outcome of our efforts to address the deficiencies of American schooling will be determined to a large extent by how we pose the problems. If you navigate by the wrong stars, pulling hard on the oars still won't get you to the destination.

Especially during this brief quadrennial period of national stocktaking that attends a presidential transition, we might well examine some of the dustier assumptions on the education-reform shelves.

Most of the commonly accepted notions I discuss here bear on what many educators have persuaded themselves is the epochal choice facing school reformers: "top-down" changes—those initiated by state or federal policymakers—or "bottom-up" innovations—those designed by local districts and individual schools. But the idea that such a tidy choice can be made—indeed, that it presents "right" and "wrong" options (and you don't have to guess which side most educators line up on)—is itself a dandy example of conventional wisdom that, upon inspection, turns out to be hogwash.

ONE OF THE ABIDING STRENGTHS OF AMERICAN EDUCATION IS LOCAL CONTROL. Though we still have upwards of 15,000 local school systems, the education action has shifted to the states: for a decade, their share of the nation's public-school dollar has exceeded the local portion. And nearly all the boldest changes in the 1980s—Tennessee's career ladder, South Carolina's comprehensive reform act, California's new curricula, Minnesota's school choice law, New Jersey's "educational bankruptcy" scheme, to cite only a few examples—have been statewide policy shifts.

While local governance and financing of schools worked satisfactorily in an agrarian society, it is less suited to a mobile, megalopolitan nation. Local politics are apt to be petty, given to patronage and favoritism. And reliance on local revenues invites allegations of fiscal inequity. The result has been, and will surely continue to be, ever-greater state dominance of education finance and regulation.

Holding individual schools to account for their performance is a good idea. So is conferring more authority on parents. But the county board of education and town superintendent's office are vestiges of the last century that may not be needed at all in the next one.

POLITICIANS SHOULD KEEP THEIR GRIMY PAWS OFF THE SCHOOLS.
Since the turn of the century, civic wisdom has held that education should
be left to the experts—professional educators and lay governing boards,
many of them appointed to their positions so as to insulate them from the
hurly-burly of electoral politics. Governor and legislator, mayor and select-
man—this seedy lot should stick to road building, waste disposal, and law
enforcement.

That arrangement got us into the fix we're in. Educators attended mainly
to their own interests. The lay boards deferred to their professional staffs, in
many places lost the ability to attract first-rate members, and wearied of the
interminable meetings and a surfeit of detail. The schools decayed.

Today, education is the largest item in the budget of every state and most
localities, and taxpayers have begun to hold elected officials responsible for the
effective use of these immense resources. As a result, many governors have
made education their issue—and some mayors are starting to do the same.

Though many educators still yearn for the old pattern, practically
everybody else now acknowledges that the proper duties of elected officials
include—along with finding resources for public education—setting standards, creating accountability systems, and charting policy for schools. The
education system, we've learned, is not self-correcting.

Policy-driven reforms of the sort that legislatures enact will not yield
authentic improvement in education and may make it worse. What is needed
instead is *restructuring*—empowering school "professionals" to make key
decisions.

It is true that outstanding schools nearly always display homegrown
qualities that cannot be mandated from on high, and imaginative experiments under way in half a dozen communities are modifying timeworn
practices in an effort to clone excellent schools.

But with some 83,000 public schools in the land, we cannot suppose that
most students would benefit if their "school team" suddenly gained greater
autonomy. Too many team members just don't have what it takes, and too
few really want to change their ways.

While the capacity for improvement may be nurtured in such schools over
time, the best approach is to alter the rules by which the system operates.
And that is the proper work of lawmakers.

NATIONAL STANDARDS FOR EDUCATION ARE UN-AMERICAN. We probably do not want federal regulations to enforce them, but perhaps the single most valuable action that George Bush could take as "education president" would be to catalyze a national consensus-seeking process, meant to settle on some basic education norms for all young Americans.

What is the minimum that a high school graduate should know and be able to do? Why should Missoula have a different standard from Malden? States, districts, and individual schools may add to the core, but in this mobile society, yesterday's fifth grader in Oregon is apt to be tomorrow's high school student in Delaware.

Youngsters across the land already watch the same movies and television programs, listen to the same music, read (if at all) the same publications, and chow down in identical outlets of the same fast-food chains. And the school curriculum is already similar in many districts, thanks to education schools, professional associations, textbook publishers, and test-makers. Why not turn this creeping sameness into a virtue? Why not have uniform minimum standards too?

TEACHING TO THE TEST DENATURES THE TEACHER-STUDENT RELATIONSHIP, PARALYZES THE CURRICULUM, AND TURNS GOALS INTO CEILINGS. If a standardized test faithfully appraises the skills and knowledge that the school system seeks to impart—if it is properly aligned with the curriculum—then there is nothing wrong with teaching to it. While schools must not coach students on actual exam items, drilling them on the array of skills and knowledge the test will probe is fine.

The tests do not have to be the multiple-choice, machine-readable variety. As has long been the case with Advanced Placement exams, they can involve analytic essays and complex problem solving. They can entail subtle computer interactions. They can even be oral. But some means are required to find out whether students have actually learned what the education system sought to teach them. Or else there is no accountability.

AT-RISK CHILDREN ARE THE CHIEF PROBLEM FACING EDUCATION. The reigning wisdom holds that the school system is drowning in a demographic tidal wave of immigrant and minority youngsters; children from impoverished, broken, and disorganized families; and students with masses of social, economic, medical, nutritional, and emotional problems. In this situation, we are told, "it is unrealistic to think of reading Shakespeare."

To be sure, growing numbers of such children are showing up at the schoolhouse door. And the persistence of an "underclass" is as vexing a social-policy problem as any we face.

But schools as presently constituted have scant leverage over the lives of students, who typically spend less than 10 percent of their time in them, even if they attend faithfully until their 18th birthdays. And schools are good at only a few things: imparting cognitive skills and knowledge and—sometimes—boosting sound values, good behavior, and physical fitness.

The tangled problems of at-risk youngsters have their origins outside the schools and seldom can be solved inside them, though it is legitimate to enlist the schools in whatever policy partnerships are formed. To pretend otherwise is to raise false hopes.

But there is one aspect of the at-risk problem that educators alone can do something about and should be held accountable for: the risk of attending a lousy school.

For no one does a first-rate school make a bigger difference than the disadvantaged child. And dozens of schools succeed magnificently, even in the most woebegone locales and with the most challenging of youngsters. Such examples offer plain proof that schools can be islands of order and learning in a tempestuous social sea. What we need are thousands more such places.

The assumption that high standards and a meaty curriculum are bad for disadvantaged youngsters is a recipe for continued second-class citizenship. Anyone who cares about equal opportunity has got to note with alarm that among black and Hispanic high school graduates in 1987, only 23 and 21 percent respectively had taken a course menu including at least four years of English and three years each of mathematics, science, and social studies. For whites, the figure was 30 percent; for Asians, 52 percent. Better schools are going to cost more.

The expenditures of American public schools have been rising in real terms for decades and this year are the highest ever—in the vicinity of $4,800 per pupil, or about $110,000 for every classroom. The biggest problem is not that we're spending too little but that the return on this huge investment is too skimpy.

Yes, a few needed changes will demand still more money. Lengthening the school day and year, for example, are big-ticket items. Sophisticated testing methods cost more than the simple kind. But good textbooks cost no more than bad ones; algebra and history are no more expensive to teach than consumer math and family living; at $50,000 a head, enough money is already being paid to high school principals to hire good ones. And significant sums can be saved—as Chicago may soon demonstrate—by sharp reductions in the bureaucracy of the superintendent's office.

> **CHOICE IS JUST A CODE WORD FOR VOUCHERS, WHICH PORTEND THE END OF PUBLIC EDUCATION AS WE KNOW IT.** The private school aid debates of earlier years have nearly vanished from the policy arena; the center-ring event today is choice within public education. Such approaches as magnet schools, alternative schools, and schools-within-schools have proved hugely successful in settings as dissimilar, for example, as Spanish Harlem; Cambridge, Massachusetts; and Prince George's County, Maryland.

Choice is now also expanding to the state level. The Minnesota legislature voted in 1988 to give every youngster in the state the right to attend any of its public schools. New York's commissioner of education, Thomas Sobol, recently proposed that any child in the state should be able to transfer from a bad school to one that works; California's superintendent of public instruction, Bill Honig, is heading in the same direction.

The choice issue illuminates the folly of polarizing the reform debate into top-down and bottom-up strategies. As professional teams in individual schools begin to decide what will be taught, how, and by whom, schools will come to differ. It is only right that children and parents be able to select the ones that suit them: the more such "building-level autonomy"—that is, bottom-up reform—is exercised, the more important it is that families be allowed to match the educational needs of their children to the varied offerings of schools in their communities.

Yet replacing involuntary pupil assignments with choice among schools is the quintessential policymakers' decision. However logical a corollary it is to bottom-up reform, the principle of choice cannot be installed from the building level. It needs a gutsy superintendent, a crusading governor, a cadre of bold legislators—and it needs policy control over a lot of schools or it doesn't make any sense at all.

Neither, however, does it make much sense to offer choice in a tightly regulated system of virtually identical schools. What then is to choose?

Only when schools are encouraged to differ—and when educators and officials are willing to live with the certainty that some will thrive and others wither—is choice among schools an authentic reform. This means forging the softer metals associated with bottom-up school improvement on the steel policy anvil of the top-down strategy.

We are not dealing with a neat dichotomy after all. Nor is most of the rest of today's conventional wisdom about education reform more than a collection of half-truths, none of them able to bear much weight until the missing parts are located and firmly joined.

Chester E. Finn Jr., former assistant secretary for educational research and improvement in the U.S. Education Department, is a senior fellow at the Hoover Institution at Stanford University and president of the Thomas B. Fordham Foundation in Washington, D.C.

My basic views, embodied in the Coalition of Essential Schools' 10 Common
Principles, have, at their core, not changed. The early 2000s are not the 1980s,
of course, and my personal take on contemporary high school reform has
adapted accordingly. The application of those principles has twisted and turned
over the years, but to my eye their philosophical core remains persuasively
relevant. The Coalition of Essential Schools' vigorous and thoughtful growth
and the continuous "reinvention" of its work by its current, able Oakland,
California-based staff, gives me enormous satisfaction. I am a lucky retiree!—TRS

PUBLISHED JUNE 25, 1997

ON LAME HORSES AND TORTOISES

[THEODORE R. SIZER]

A recent issue of *Education Week* had a page-one story headlined "Teachers
Need Nuts, Bolts of Reforms, Experts Say" (April 30, 1997). The article quotes
a teacher: "There is no model for me to make a prediction about. How can we
put into practice a design that has not been developed, explained, or modeled
for us?" An expert is quoted: "It is unfair and unrealistic to expect America's
overburdened teachers to reinvent their roles and redesign their organizations without providing explicit and proven means of doing so." The article
goes on to report that "one of the programs that have taken the heaviest hits

for providing schools with only vague reform principles is the Coalition of Essential Schools." An expert is quoted as saying that "perhaps less than 5 percent of elementary or secondary schools in the entire country . . . have the capacity to translate reform guided by general principles into reality."

Good grief.

Have we been backing a lame horse? Apparently so, some authorities think. Our sin is that we don't *prescribe*. Teachers, it has seemed to some others over the last couple of decades, are to put the bolts in at the right times and at the correct rate, all according to someone else's plan. Outsiders will then find a test or, better yet, make one up that fits their specific agenda, teach the teachers to drill the kids at meeting it, and—presto!—we have "reform." The children, well drilled, do well on the test—and test scores are the name of the educational game. We thereby have "proof" that the children are truly educated, ready to take on the 21st century.

However, it is unworthy to parody such an argument, however tempting it may be. The stakes are too high.

To my eye, the give-'em-the-nuts-and-bolts strategy is a very threadbare conception of reform. Our objective should be a child's deep understanding of the world and a habitual readiness to act effectively on that understanding. Our strategy, therefore, should focus not only on what a child can do in an immediate testing situation but equally on the intellectual habits that youngster develops. Kids have to know things and perform basic academic operations, yes; but they ultimately have to be able to use those skills, to *understand* and to be in the habit of such understanding. It is not enough to know about Lewis and Clark. Students need to understand why they did what they did and why Jefferson sponsored them, to connect this, say, to the convictions lying behind the National Aeronautics and Space Administration, and to ponder humankind's willingness to take huge risks to satisfy a yen to explore in a disciplined, sustained way. Youngsters need to understand risk-takers' dreams and perhaps be inspired by them.

Tightly orchestrated routines lead poorly toward the teaching of habits. Habits—the willingness to use one's mind well when no one is looking— spring from incentives that require nurturing, one unique student at a time. Good teachers know this. Parents with some money dig deep in their pockets to pay for just this service in private schools, and those with children at affluent public schools insist on it. Such personalization is damnably "in-efficient." It is also inescapable, given the differences among students. And "thinking well by habit" emerges gradually, peeking out here and there. Every day must be test day.

All this does not mean that every teacher starts from scratch with every child. *Of course* no one should have to reinvent the wheel. That is why the Coalition of Essential Schools has gone to extravagant lengths to connect teachers and schools for the sharing of all sorts of ideas and "models"—as good examples. That is why we publish our newsletter, *Horace,* and have materials such as the exhibitions collection widely available. That is why we have a fall forum, which is a massive swap shop. That is why I wrote and published *Horace's School* and *Horace's Hope.* That is why books by Donna Muncey, Patrick McQuillan, Joe McDonald, Patricia Wasley, and others have been sponsored by the Coalition of Essential Schools. That is why the coali-tion's e-mail traffic grows exponentially. We have at hand honest stories of the process of change, endless examples of real student work for us to pon-der. All these challenge us, inform us, open our eyes. This activity of sharing our work, provoking each other with it, is different, however, from telling us precisely what we ought to do.

I hope we can resist the newly rediscovered old Progressive trick of im-posed, systematic "reform," where "success" is measured primarily, even ex-clusively, by one sort or another of standardized test, where the route to high "scores" is wholly orchestrated from outside the school, and where the worth of a child and of a school is ultimately judged on the basis of such profoundly limited scores. We need systems of accountability far more subtle, humble, and fair than that. Good teaching and learning are rarely linear, neat, pre-dictable. The serendipities and distractions and fascinations that crowd into every classroom (if students are allowed to raise their heads) conspire against that. Learning and therefore teaching are messy, but messy does not mean bad any more than orderly means good.

What also bothers me about the argument that "we" (whoever that is) need to tell teachers (and parents) in detail what to do is its short-sightedness. Training up teachers to carry out something that someone else has fully devel-oped gives those teachers no experience in matching their work to the learning of their particular students. Further, that "something" will itself be transient (if history is any guide), meaning that today's remedy may be scotched tomorrow. A faculty unskilled in handling for itself the most important elements of its work will be incapable of moving responsibly with the times.

But, the argument goes, the teachers are "overburdened," and thus must let outside experts do their curricular and pedagogical thinking for them. Yes, teachers are overburdened: Horace has had to compromise too much. Maybe, however, the remedy for this condition is to lessen the burden rather than to take decisions away from teachers. Especially in secondary schools, this usually requires substantial shifting (usually the limiting) of priorities, bringing the student load per teacher down to a level where serious teaching can happen. We in the Coalition know both that such can be done and that it is distressingly difficult to accomplish, even if the need for the rearrangements is blatantly obvious. But it can be done, when authorities have had the backbone to support significant restructuring. It has been done. And the kids show the benefit.

There should be three questions for those intent upon the reform and assessment of schooling. First, are the criteria and instruments for the assessment of children, schools, and school systems clear, unequivocally fair, and demonstrably correlated with likely useful intellectual activity in the students' future lives? (If not, don't administer them.) Second, have the systems (administrations and unions) of which the schools and children are a part provided the necessary conditions for effective work and guaranteed stability to pursue it? (If not, get on with that reform, or change the way the "system," so obviously stuck, is controlled.) Third, has each school seized the opportunity provided by that new structure to teach well, and do the children reflect that powerful teaching? (If not, help the school; and if this does not work, shut it down.) All three questions are necessary to ask. They work together—we all know, for example, the justified fury we feel when someone else mocks us for not teaching at once, say, 150 distracted adolescents to write well in groups of 35 meeting for snippets of time over the course of a week, or when a child we know well is "given" scores which do not reflect her competence or incompetence.

Most repellent to me in the line of argument reported in *Education Week* is the clear, if implicit, assumption that teachers cannot be trusted with their own craft. There is a self-fulfilling prophecy here, of course; impose routines on a job, thus trivializing it, and those who hold that job will act accordingly—that is, doing that work and no more, "working to the rule." Most important, many good folk will avoid the profession, or leave it early. What well-educated person wants a career that belittles his or her integrity and authority?

We are told that only 5 percent of the schools have the capacity to reform themselves. One wonders from where this extraordinary number comes. But let it be. I suppose that British generals in the late 1770s said the same sorts of things about the colonials' rabble army.

I recently watched a stunning performance of *Antigone* staged by seventh, eighth, and ninth graders. It had the awkwardnesses of that age, but it displayed its wonderfully aware exuberance too. At the play's end, the audience stayed put and the cast remained on stage, allowing talk across some 200 folk of all ages about the play and what it meant. Did the actors "merely act," or did they "become their characters"? The students' description of their shift from "following direction" to "becoming" Creon or Antigone showed remarkable understanding, powerful empathy. They themselves struggled with the dilemmas that are the heart of the play, dilemmas that speak intensely to our own times. They were learning well.

This kind of deep, complex work does not arise from prescripted scenarios. It emerges from the entwining of particular people, old and young, with particular ideas. *Antigone worked* with this group of youngsters. At another time and with another group of kids, the director might have chosen another drama. Only the people on the spot would know what might be best. This *Antigone* was as respectful as it was demanding, representative of the heart of powerful secondary education. The understanding achieved is fuel for the next challenge. And that understanding remains in part mysterious, difficult to define, even more difficult to measure. It is unlikely to be provoked in kids by robot teachers. And it is not that teachers don't have access to the "material": The play *Antigone* has been there for us to use, in one form or another, for 2,500 years.

We remove the immediate and particular quality from schooling at our peril. Those very nuts and bolts—the "regularities" of schooling—are what catch or repel, interest or bore, youngsters. Kids of all income levels dream and are ripe for inspiration. The adults closest to the children are the most important in coaching the demanding work—the critical nuts and bolts—that follows upon inspiration, child by child. These adults must be powerful, authoritative, and not "overburdened" people. They cannot dodge these decisions and serve the children well. Force them to teach someone else's prescribed plan and you cheapen them. Persist in the forcing and the teaching force will shrivel in commitment and imagination.

Devices for quick "indicators" of learning have their attraction. However, they are the tactic of the hare, looking for a quick and decisive solution. But building communities of responsible people is slow work, worthy of the tortoise. Only the schools that arise from such careful crafting will provide students who possess the powerful and often subtle learnings required in our modern society. The Coalition of Essential Schools, and others who espouse this philosophy, must never apologize for being a tortoise.

Theodore R. Sizer is founder and chairman emeritus of the Coalition of Essential Schools. He was dean of the Harvard Graduate of Education during the 1960s; headmaster of Phillips Academy, Andover, during the 1970s; and professor of education at Brown University during the 1980s. He now is university professor emeritus at Brown. During the 1990s and with his wife, Nancy, he was one of the founders of the Francis W. Parker Charter Essential School in Devens, Massachusetts, and served, again jointly with Nancy, as the school's acting co-principal during the Parker School's second year. The Sizers are currently associated with the Twin Cities Collaborative, a school reform initiative based at Fitchburg State College in central Massachusetts.

Since we wrote this article, little has changed. If there's any ray of hope, it is an increasing interest in creating high schools with majors, or clusters, or schools-within-schools, or (in the latest terminology) "pathways" with some kind of theme or focus. These themes are often broadly occupational, such as business, health, or biotechnology. In some schools, pathways look more "academic," with themes such as communications arts, arts and humanities, computer partnerships, and ecology. These are promising options that restructure high schools in fundamental ways, but they still have to battle with older concepts that never seem to die.—WNG and ML

PUBLISHED SEPTEMBER 22, 2004

IS THE COMPREHENSIVE HIGH SCHOOL DOOMED?

[**W. NORTON GRUBB & MARVIN LAZERSON**]

The rise and fall of the public comprehensive high school is one of the great tragedies of American education. When it took form in the first decades of the 20th century, the high school embodied enormous expectations: preparing youths for a labor market that offered serious jobs, facilitating access to college, and channeling the Sturm und Drang of adolescence into productive forms of citizenship.

The comprehensive high school was a uniquely American phenomenon. It sought to gather all youths into a single institution that would prepare them for different roles, in workplaces, in civic life, in families and communities. It was of course suffused with stereotypical assumptions and invidious discriminations. The primary occupational preparation of girls was assumed to be domestic science and, later, secretarial training; African Americans were prepared for manual labor; many immigrant youths were thought genetically incapable of preparing for college. These assumptions all reinforced conditions of inequality that existed outside the schools. But the historical success of the high school in educating nearly all 14- to 17-year-olds and in providing genuine opportunities to overcome invidious distinctions has been substantial. Through much of the 20th century, it stood as the centerpiece of America's educational system, the embodiment of the American Dream of getting ahead through schooling.

No one would make that claim today. The comprehensive high school is a blighted institution, with its academic purpose reduced to preparing some students for vocational study in college, and its direct vocational role eliminated by the collapse of the youth labor market. It is now a place to warehouse young people until they move on to somewhere else.

WHAT HAPPENED? A century ago, the high school was primarily an academic institution, in the specific sense that its curriculum was dominated by academic subjects and in the more disparaging sense that formal schooling was distant from the political, community, and economic life outside its doors. The dominance of academic subjects gave way under pressure to vocationalize the curriculum, to prepare students directly for entry-level jobs that traditionally did not require secondary schooling. The vocational education movement changed the high school, as trade and industrial training, secretarial and clerical preparation, home economics, agricultural education, and all the mechanisms of tracking became routine.

But the broader significance of vocational education lay in its role in transforming the conception of schooling into one of getting all students better jobs, not just those in vocational education. What we call the American system of vocationalism came to dominate all segments of schooling, from the high school to the university, so that the only real measuring rod was whether the schooling moved individuals into better jobs.

Through the first half of the 20th century, the public comprehensive high school continued to look like a good bet. Suburban expansion was based in part on the hope for better schools, to help young people get ahead. Then the bottom seemed to fall out. In the 1950s, competition with the Soviet Union led to attacks on low academic standards. The 1960s saw unruly youths demand civil rights. The 1970s witnessed sharp criticism over the high school's isolation from the world of adults and the world of work. The 1980s returned to 1950s-style attacks on low academic standards, followed by two decades of attempts to raise standards while everyone scrambled to find yet other cures. At century's end, what had once been viewed as the strongest part of the education system had become its weakest link.

> **WHY DID IT HAPPEN?** The deterioration occurred for many reasons, but a primary one was the virtual disappearance of a labor market for youths. The jobs that now exist for high school graduates are dreary—with low wages in a world of conspicuous consumption, no security, no benefits, no career ladders, requiring no training and little literacy since they have been dumbed down. For high school dropouts, the situation is even worse.

Staying in school in order to go to college is another matter. In the last decades of the century, economic returns to college graduation relative to high school graduation grew substantially. Those with two-year associate's degrees also do substantially better than high school graduates, though not as well as those with baccalaureate degrees.

Almost all discussions about secondary education today involve the reality that its only real purpose is to facilitate college entry. And within that mandate, serious concerns with learning exist only among those few students, perhaps 5 percent to 10 percent, who aspire to highly selective colleges. For the rest, the academic curriculum is something to be endured; the goal is simply to accumulate credits and a minimal grade point average to get into some college. The overwhelming majority of undergraduate colleges and universities are not especially competitive, since they accept 80 percent to 90 percent of applicants, and the community colleges, which now enroll almost 50 percent of all entering freshmen, are open to anyone who wants to enter.

The vocational curriculum is no longer serious, as it has become small and fragmented. It focuses on low-level jobs without any real benefits in employment, and students drift through with low aspirations. What is euphemistically referred to as the general track, with "life skills" and watered-down "academic" courses for students likely to enter unskilled jobs, has never offered serious options, from the time it was labeled "Life Adjustment" after World War II to the present.

Most students meander through high school with no clear ideas about the future, caught between the belief that finishing will get them better jobs and the fact that there is no longer any obvious connection between staying in school and the labor market—other than "going to college." The students hoping for vocational training get virtually none. Most teachers and counselors now preach "college for all," partly because they fear being charged with tracking students, but in the process furthering the sense that college is the only goal.

Most students have become disengaged from learning of any sort. They believe that getting a degree will help them, but they do not associate that achievement with learning, at least not what schools have to teach. What counts in the labor market is the quantity of schooling an individual has completed, not the quality of learning, so students have an incentive to continue as long as possible without expending more than the minimum amount of effort to pass. This leads to overeducation, or more accurately, overschooling, in which students get more schooling than they need for the jobs they are likely to get. But even the incentive simply to stay in school doesn't work. For some, the level of disengagement is so high that they drop out before graduation. Despite the century-long hope of "high school for all," dropout rates are high, between 25 percent and 30 percent nationally, and considerably worse in urban districts and for minority students, where they run as high as 50 percent to 60 percent. And despite the efforts of the standards movement to invigorate learning and academic achievement in the high schools, little has been accomplished.

{ **WHAT CAN WE DO?** The future need not be all doom and gloom. There are innovations developing that could help. Efforts to reconstitute high schools as small communities with a clear sense of purpose and with something serious to accomplish in their own right can be encouraged. Large comprehensive high schools are a disaster—chaotic, fragmented, purposeless factories. In contrast, schools-within-schools, theme-based schools, charter schools, magnet schools, and schools where teachers stay with their students as they progress hold out some hope that common purposes, built on a community of learners, can restore coherence, engagement, and motivation.

One example includes programs that we call *education through occupations*. These emphasize broad occupational areas, elastic enough to encompass standard academic subjects and to integrate occupational content as well. The "college and careers" approach, as University of California, Berkeley, professor David Stern calls it, can prepare students in the same program for college and for employment and future work responsibilities.

Academic learning and school experiences can also be connected to life outside the school—through student projects, service learning, environmental protection, work-based internships, and co-op placements. These are hard to establish and harder to maintain at a high level of learning aligned with in-school instruction. But the alternative is to continue the high school as an institution cloistered from political, economic, and community life, to the detriment of students looking for something real to do.

The list of possibilities that flow from these approaches is substantial—improved guidance to clarify students' future options and their relationships to both secondary and postsecondary education, a dismantling of the inequities of the formal and informal tracking system, the integration of nontraditional teachers into secondary education. And of course there are some issues, like the poor labor market for young people, that the schools can do little about but that need serious attention from more active government.

Reconstructing the high school requires giving it some meaning of its own. If the curriculum is important only in instrumental ways, as preparation for college or later employment, then it is simply something to endure while waiting for something else. If the curriculum has no intrinsic value, calls to learn will continue to fall by the wayside, and threats to enforce learning through high-stakes tests are unlikely to do much good.

The real challenge is to tie educational standards to the world around us in ways that recast academic disciplines and vocational education. Only then will young people understand the world's richness and start formulating roles in it for themselves. Only then will the high school save itself.

W. Norton Grubb holds the David Gardner Chair in Higher Education at the University of California, Berkeley, and is faculty coordinator of the Principal Leadership Institute there.

Marvin Lazerson is professor emeritus at the University of Pennsylvania.

Grubb and Lazerson are coauthors of *The Education Gospel: The Economic Power of Schooling* (Harvard University Press, 2004).

Not much has changed. Calls for evidence-based educational policies based on well-designed studies reverberate as loudly as ever. Evidence matters. Good studies make us smarter about our educational choices, but they don't make those choices any easier. The simplicities such work often promises disappear in the wake of disagreements about research designs and statistical analyses. At the heart of these debates are fundamental clashes of values and priorities. They translate into battles over which instruments to use, which participants to count, and who gets compared to whom and for how long. No experiment will satisfy everyone; even the composition of review panels becomes politicized. But the alternatives are worse. So collect evidence, expect complexity—and deal with it.—LSS

PUBLISHED JUNE 8, 2005

SEEK SIMPLICITY . . . AND DISTRUST IT

[LEE S. SHULMAN]

Alfred North Whitehead's dictum about the virtues and dangers of simplicity helps explain why we are confused about what kind of evidence should be used to guide education policy. We often have lots of evidence to choose from; the problem is making sense of it and drawing the right lessons. Let's look at some examples.

Educational researchers David C. Berliner and Audrey L. Amrein, both from Arizona State University, published in 2002 a report called *The Impact of High-Stakes Tests on Student Academic Performance.* They concluded that such testing failed to have the intended positive impact on student learning and was often bad for students. The *New York Times* ran the story on page one. The *Times'* editorial page, as well as others nationwide, featured the research and urged caution on the implementation of high-stakes testing. The editorial expressed particular concerns over the testing included in the federal No Child Left Behind Act, through which schools can be financially penalized if test scores show that they are "in need of improvement." It was a great story and an important one. Research evidence had thrown a serious wrench into the very heart of the Bush (and Clinton) school reform strategies. Or had it?

A week later, economists Martin Carnoy and Susanna Loeb of Stanford University reported their own findings from a similar database (since published in the journal *Educational Evaluation and Policy Analysis*) and, using different methods of analysis, concluded that Berliner and Amrein got it wrong: high-stakes testing actually was pretty good for kids. A month later, Margaret E. Raymond and Eric A. Hanushek of the Hoover Institution published their own analysis and concluded that high-stakes testing was actually *very* good for kids. They used much the same data as Berliner, Carnoy, and their respective colleagues, but analyzed it differently, aggregated the information at different levels, and drew conclusions quite different from Berliner and Amrein's and reasonably congruent with Carnoy and Loeb's.

These contradictions motivated statistician Henry Braun of the Educational Testing Service to conduct a new study in which he used four different modes of analysis to evaluate the data on the connections between statewide high-stakes testing and student achievement. He concluded that the decisions that researchers made about methods of analysis largely determined which kinds of findings they reported. Analyzed in some ways, the evidence showed positive effects for high-stakes testing; analyzed in other ways, there was no discernible effect.

I happen to know personally most of the players in this drama. They are all serious scholars, careful quantitative analysts, and passionate educators. They reported evidence instead of anecdote or opinion. And they disagreed wildly. What's a policymaker (or parent, for that matter) to do, especially when we are urged to engage in "evidence-based education"?

A similar conundrum emerged a couple of years ago when a research team from Harvard University, led by political science professor Paul E. Peterson, announced the results of a carefully designed *experimental* study concluding that school vouchers work to raise academic achievement for poor kids. (The high-stakes-testing studies were not experiments; they were post-hoc analyses of existing databases from the states.) The Harvard team's claims were challenged by critics, including some of their own collaborators from the policy-research firm Mathematica. The folks from Mathematica cautioned that all we can conclude from this study is that vouchers worked positively for sixth grade African-American boys in New York City. In fact, only if the scores for all the kids in these studies are combined, including those of the African-American sixth graders, would there be a statistically significant benefit for the voucher group. A columnist in the *Wall Street Journal* attacked the critics, arguing that as long as there was an overall positive effect and no evidence that vouchers were harmful to anyone, it made sense to proceed with this policy initiative.

Evidence is supposed to make life easier, or at least more rational, for policymakers in education. Instead of battling over ideologies, we are urged to conduct careful research, design real experiments whenever possible, collect data, and then dispassionately draw our conclusions. Would that the world were that simple. Truth is, research is all about exercising judgment under conditions of uncertainty, and even experimental designs don't relieve us of those judgmental burdens. The acts of designing experiments themselves involve value judgments, and interpreting the results always demands careful judgment. As the late pioneer in educational psychology Lee Cronbach often observed, even a carefully designed experiment is ultimately a case study, conducted with particular teachers and students, in particular places at a particular time. And the analysis of all studies depends heavily on the analytic methods used, the level at which the data are aggregated and either combined or separated, and the interpretive powers and predilections of the scholars.

For the same reasons that jury members and Supreme Court justices often disagree with one another, and appeals courts often reverse the judgments of lower courts, evidence alone never tells the story. This is not a problem unique to education or the social sciences. Economists battle over whether lowering taxes stimulates the economy more than it increases deficits, and each side offers evidence. In medicine, cancer researchers give competing interpretations of studies on the efficacy of different kinds of mastectomies, and therefore of the value of alternative treatments. Surgeons disagree about the relative value of surgical versus medical interventions for treatment of atherosclerosis. From global warming to diet and nutrition, scientists conduct studies, offer evidence, and disagree about practical or policy implications.

Does this mean that evidence is irrelevant and research is unnecessary? Does it mean that education policy cannot be based on careful research? Not at all. But we need to give up the fantasy that any single study will resolve major questions. We need to recognize that research evidence rarely speaks directly to the resolution of policy controversies without the necessary mediating agencies of human judgment, human values, and a community of scholars and actors prepared to deliberate and weigh alternatives in a world of uncertainty. Researchers in education (and in most other fields) are rarely neutral. Advocates cite evidence and research. Researchers themselves often are advocates. Indeed, it's not very interesting for scholars to pursue studies of issues they don't give a damn about.

So whose evidence should we believe? Let me propose a few preliminary guidelines for adjudicating the claims and counterclaims of conflicting studies.

First, I would live by the motto "Seek simplicity . . . and distrust it." It is nearly unimaginable that any one study would support a simple policy conclusion, across the board. If a study claims to demonstrate that "bilingual education doesn't work" or that "all high-stakes testing is bad for kids," or that "phonics is the only way to learn to read," don't trust the claim. Most studies of complex policy issues yield results that are themselves complex; they must be interpreted with caution and nuance. In the study of tuition vouchers, for example, the actual findings were highly variable in terms of effects on kids by race, grade, and location. Simple conclusions emerged only if we totally ignored all the variations and seriously oversimplified the findings.

It isn't that simplicity is unachievable. The preponderance of the evidence on the value of holding back children who "fail" first grade appears to be both overwhelming and clear: holding kids back is educationally worthless. But that's a simple conclusion that comes from more than a decade of quite different studies, and in particular circumstances involving particular kids, the best judgment may well be otherwise.

Second, I would give greater credence to any study that was conducted by either investigators who had no discernible stake in the results or—even better—those whose findings run counter to their own values, tastes, and preferences. As Judge David S. Tatel of the U.S. Court of Appeals for the District of Columbia Circuit observed last year, it is very difficult for the courts to take social-science research evidence seriously when it often appears that the scientists doing the research have a political or ideological stake in the desired results.

If conflict of interest is a problem with pharmaceutical research, it is certainly an impediment with educational research as well. In some cases, investigators have a long and public record of advocating for one of the results they offer evidence to support. In other cases, their prior preferences are either unknown or unformed. As we typically do in qualitative studies, we should expect investigators to put their values, preferences, and commitments on the table when they offer their evidence and interpretations. It's unrealistic to expect that every important study will be conducted by scholars who are disinterested in the findings. We need to go further to increase the credibility of evidence.

Third, I would insist that every major study with policy significance undergo serious peer review before its findings and the policy interpretations associated with them are trumpeted to the media. The review should deal with at least three aspects of the study: How well does the design and analysis permit the claims being made for the interpretation of the data? What other studies offer both complementary and contradictory findings, and how does this study compare with them? And perhaps most important, even if the findings of the research meet the strict canons of scholarly work in one's discipline, how reasonable are the claims based on the evidence of this study to support the more general policy claims now being put forward?

Each of the three studies on high-stakes testing did undertake forms of peer review, at least with respect to a substantial chunk of the evidence they each presented. But peer review is not a universal process. Current modes of peer review for journals are unbearably slow. Therefore, we need a much swifter mechanism for such critical appraisals if this proposal is realistic. How can a serious form of review precede high-profile press releases and press conferences and yet not unacceptably impede dissemination?

Fourth, I would remind investigators that they have a social responsibility to act as "stewards" of their fields. They are responsible not only to zealously conduct their own studies and to organize the rhetoric to support their claims, but they also must, like lawyers, be "officers of the court" who bear responsibility for the fidelity of their work to the integrity of their field. They should so organize their studies that there is someone designated whose role and responsibility is to examine the procedures, data, and interpretations, and ask, How might it be otherwise? How consistent with the findings is an interpretation opposite to that offered by the study directors? In many European countries, all doctoral dissertations are defended publicly, with the participation of a formal "antagonist" whose job is to challenge the findings of the study.

A research study needs someone whose job it is to ask how susceptible the evidence and its interpretation are to intelligent (or just plain politically motivated) criticism. In fact, journalists have a professional obligation to be more critical in vetting stories of research before they publish them, to ask about peer review and about the questions raised by the research critics.

The bottom line is that we must move to a more evidence-based strategy for crafting our education policies, but we cannot pretend that there are some forms of research—even controlled experiments—that are guaranteed to provide answers to our questions without requiring the exercise of expert judgment and structured peer review. Evidence informs and enlightens decision making; it does not bypass the need for interpretation and judgment. It's unrealistic to expect that educational research will regularly be conducted by those who have absolutely no stake in the outcomes. Education is not, and never will be, a values-free zone. Nevertheless, we need ways to review research findings, evaluate the evidence, consider the values inherent in the situation, and render judgments that our citizenry can trust.

Beyond these proposals, I would recommend the formation of a new policy forum to assist in regularly reviewing and evaluating policy-relevant educational research. In some areas we may need the equivalent of research-review SWAT teams that can be called in on a regular basis to review competing claims and the evidence that supports them. In other cases, the use of "consensus panels" can be quite useful in the face of complex, multiple studies with a range of findings, interpretations, and policy recommendations, though the pace of their efforts can be snail-like.

The National Research Council of the National Academies might well take the lead in such an activity, assisted by a range of both self-consciously partisan and intentionally nonpartisan bodies. Such forums would organize quick-response review panels and also conduct periodic reviews when serious policy controversies arise. The forum should be nongovernmental, to avoid conflicts of interest with the education policy missions of any federal, state, or local government. (The current swirl of controversy around the Bush administration's implementation of the No Child Left Behind program exemplifies this problem.)

If we can follow those guidelines, there will remain big, unanswered questions about the impact of high-stakes testing on the achievement of elementary school kids, and about the value of vouchers to reduce educational inequality. But we will have much more confidence in the value of the evidence put forward to help us traverse the thickets of education policy. I can assure you, however, that the picture that emerges from the evidence won't likely be simple. That's not necessarily a problem with the quality of the research; it may simply be a characteristic of the world in which we live.

Lee S. Shulman is president of the Carnegie Foundation for the Advancement
of Teaching in Stanford, California, and Charles E. Ducommun
Professor of Education Emeritus at Stanford University.

PART EIGHT

CHARTERS
AND CHOICE

Eighteen years after writing this essay, I would change some of the details of
implementation, but the principles seem as sound to me now as they did when I wrote
this piece: line up authority with accountability, get the benefits of competition while
not losing any of the advantages of public schools, and create as many opportunities
as possible for our school professionals to show what they can really do when they
get the chance, but in an environment of sound standards and measures set by
the state, with clear rewards for performance and penalties for failure.—MST

PUBLISHED JUNE 21, 1989

CREATING AN ENTREPRENEURIAL SCHOOL SYSTEM

[MARC S. TUCKER]

Most of the discussion about accountability these days seems curiously vacuous.

Many school people see accountability as a process of accounting—telling
the public how funds were spent and how the system and the students perform against a set of indicators.

But the public thinks in quite different terms: If students are not learning, who is responsible and what happens to them?

At the same time, discussion of restructuring has for the most part
focused on individual schools, not districts. The relation of restructuring

The views expressed in this essay, adapted from a book, do not necessarily represent the
views of the National Center on Education and the Economy's board of trustees.

to what happens in the district as a whole has been largely dealt with by references to "school-based management": the job of the district is to make restructuring possible by pushing decisions now made at the central office level down to the schools, to the professionals in closest contact with the students.

But if it stops there, this view of restructuring has little chance of working. Until the public is satisfied that teachers and principals will take full responsibility for the results of their decisions, it is not likely to regard them as true professionals or grant them the major voice in how students get educated.

There must be explicit rewards for performance and penalties for failure. *Performance* itself must be defined, and it must be measurable. And because most elementary and secondary education is a public function, the community as a whole must agree on standards of performance—though school professionals should be active participants in the discussion.

In my view, the key to overall improvement lies in devising an approach to restructuring that centers on entire districts and includes accountability measures as an integral component.

What follows is a proposal that incorporates these features as vital elements in an "entrepreneurial" system of education, in which school staffs would have strong incentives to produce gains for their students and to operate at maximum efficiency.

Assume that the state government and the local school board have formulated a comprehensive but parsimonious set of dimensions for student performance—definitions of what a student should know and be able to do on graduation from high school. These might encompass everything from the ability to apply principles of physics to the problems of everyday life to an understanding of the essential characteristics of democratic institutions; from the ability to collaborate with others to the capacity to analyze historical data and write an essay that draws reasonable conclusions from that analysis.

Assume too that the district and the state have been able to develop satisfactory methods for assessing students' progress toward mastering these skills.

Imagine then that the superintendent and the board say to the district's staff members that they are free to form groups and plan programs that, in their judgment, would enable students to make rapid progress toward these objectives.

Each staff group would have to provide the full range of activities students required to meet the core objectives of the district over a period of years, but it would not need to have that full capacity within the group. It might wish to buy some specialist capacity—say, the teaching of music or laboratory science—from another group of teachers banded together to offer that service (these service groups might be located within the district or might be private groups based outside the district).

The staff units would be allotted pro rata shares of the district's resources to implement their programs, provided they satisfy two conditions: first, that they attract parents willing to enroll their children in the program; and second, that they present their program to a board of their peers, who would judge whether it meets professional standards of education. Upon passing both tests, they would be in business.

The entire district would then consist of such entrepreneurial groups, competing with one another for students. School buildings would simply be physical facilities managed as services; the fundamental unit of organization would be the entrepreneurial programs.

One group—say, a Montessori program for early-childhood education—might have several classrooms in each of several school buildings. Another—for example, a secondary-school program organized around the study of technology from a scientific, social, historical, and political point of view—might occupy all of one school building and part of another.

Embracing all students, these programs would grow or decline to the degree that they were able to attract pupils. The base budget for each would be a function of the size of the student body corrected by a weighting that took into account the characteristics of the students; non-English-speaking or physically handicapped students, for example, would bring in additional revenue. This provision, creating a stimulus for programs to attract the most capable professionals to work with the students who need them the most, is crucial.

Beyond the base budget, the district would hold a substantial portion of its overall budget in reserve for distribution at the end of the year. This reserve would be dispensed according to a unit's success in promoting student progress against the state and district measures. A program that showed major gains would receive a substantial year-end bonus.

The staff of such a program would have the option of putting that money in its pocket or plowing it back into the program's operation. It would have a strong incentive to choose the latter course, knowing that other programs would be reinvesting the funds and those that elected not to do so would be at a competitive disadvantage.

The district would decide on a student-performance "floor," below which no program would be allowed to fall. In this way, parents and taxpayers could be assured that well-meaning incompetents or charlatans could not persuade unwary or inattentive parents of the merits of a poor program. Even more important, those left behind in a program that was losing students to the competition would not be in danger of receiving a substandard education.

No group could discriminate on the basis of race, sex, handicapping condition, or limited English-speaking capacity. None could turn clients away because they did not meet entrance requirements, though a popular program could use a lottery to keep its size down if it did not wish to expand.

Within broad limits, each program staff would be free to devise its own curriculum, though its choices would be constrained by the student-performance standards set by the state and district, and by the structure of the incentive system. In effect, the staff would be free to choose the means by which students reached goals embraced by the community.

Each unit could also add its own goals to those established by the state and district. One early-elementary program, for example, might work at acquiring a reputation as a place serving the needs of parents who worked a full day; another might concentrate on attracting parents who wanted a program reflecting Piagetian principles of child growth and development. One high school unit might offer a curriculum geared to meeting the needs of the local laser industry for highly skilled technicians, and another might specialize in the arts. All programs, however, would be operating in the context of the goals that applied to all students; none could turn out narrowly trained graduates whose prospects later on in life would be constrained by the lack of a broad education.

The job of the board, the superintendent, and the central office staff in such a scheme would be to set the goals, structure the reward system, disseminate information about student performance by program to parents and community members, develop standards for hiring school staff (though the management of each group would determine who actually taught in that program), distribute funds to the programs, maintain a robust staff-development system, operate the physical facilities, and provide the necessary support services.

Some support services, like transportation, would be centrally funded and controlled. But others, such as curricular and instructional support, would be purchased by the programs in the field. They could buy those services wherever they wished—the central-office service would go out of business if it were not delivering support of a quality and at a price attractive to program managers.

The program staff could not be held accountable for student progress unless the district had a policy requiring students to remain enrolled in the school where they began the year throughout that year. In inner cities now experiencing substantial student movement between neighborhoods and schools during the year, the district would have to be prepared to bus students from wherever they move after the beginning of the year to the school in which they originally enrolled.

This is a real cost of the structure I have laid out, but it can be justified on grounds having nothing to do with the merits of my proposal. In any case, since the choice feature of this plan would require that a district transport any student to any school within its boundaries, the specific requirement to provide transportation to students whose families move during the course of the year would be only one aspect of increased transportation needs.

Perhaps the most important objective of this proposal is to create program staffs that would behave like entrepreneurial units. They would be to existing schools what Federal Express is to the Postal Service.

All students would benefit, but none—with the proposed incentive structure—more than the minority and low-income youths who fare so badly under the current system.

This plan would both demand and produce profound changes in the culture of American schools. Successful implementation would require not only great managerial and political skill but also creation of staff-development systems that simply do not yet exist in the schools.

But the benefits could be no less profound. There is every reason to believe that gains in performance would be comparable to those achieved by the Japanese managers—using methods developed in America—who took over failed American automobile plants and, with the same workers who had been there before, turned them into highly successful enterprises.

Marc S. Tucker is president of the National Center on Education and the Economy in Washington, D.C. He created the first Commission on the Skills of the American Workforce in 1989, as well as the New Commission on the Skills of the American Workforce in 2005. He is coauthor (with Judy B. Codding) of *Standards for Our Schools: How to Set Them, Measure Them, and Reach Them* (Jossey-Bass, 2002).

A decade after writing my Commentary, I am even more convinced that we must make public schools more like private without privatizing public education. Our failure to do so has resulted in 10 years of privatization schemes that continue to undermine public education. Yet I continue to believe that public schools should be overhauled, not abandoned. Through collaboration, flexibility, and depolarization of education reform debates, we can build the kind of systems and relationships that would make good schools available to all children. This cannot be accomplished through exceptions or opting out. Our real challenge remains to turn the exceptions into the norm.—AU

PUBLISHED JANUARY 31, 1996

MAKE PUBLIC SCHOOLS MORE LIKE PRIVATE

[ADAM URBANSKI]

It will take a lot to make public schools more effective for all students: greater academic rigor, higher standards of conduct, more parental involvement, stronger incentives for the students themselves, and of course more access to health and social services for the many students who are in need of such. Everyone knows this, yet some continue to call for privatization, vouchers, and other schemes that would allow parents to spend public money to send their children to private schools.

Such a defeatist approach is both irrational and unnecessary—especially since we have not yet tried to fix that which truly ails public education in this country. It confuses "helping" public schools with "dismantling" public schools. The cure would be worse than the disease. Instead of giving up on public schools altogether—which is precisely what would happen if we drained them of resources by diverting public funds to private schools—why not make public schools more like private?

What makes private schools different from public schools? Is it that they have better teachers? Hardly. Teachers in public schools are just as dedicated and often more credentialed than teachers in private schools. Better students, then? No. The fact that more public school children are poor does not mean that they are less intelligent. And while family support and readiness to learn are indeed relevant factors, they are not insurmountable hurdles—if we accelerate our efforts to coordinate education reform with reforms in health care and social services.

It seems to me that the way to make public schools more effective is to emulate some of the desirable features of private schools: small size of schools and smaller class size, less bureaucracy and fewer layers of administration, more choice and more market dynamics, and most important, the right to set and enforce high standards of conduct and academic rigor.

I believe that this can be achieved in the public school system. Here's how:

- Continue and accelerate the current drive to create smaller schools and schools-within-schools. Of course some provisions need to be made to keep the advantages of large schools, such as offering courses that only a small percentage of students want. But small schools where students are well-known are more effective. Also, by multiplying the number of available schools we would expand the number of choices for parents, students, and educators.

- Give each school increased autonomy over its own organization, budget, and staffing. Each school should also have the right to exceed (but not lower) the uniform standards for behavior codes and academic expectations. Each self-governing school would also be free to develop its own theme and its own uniqueness. Each school would be led by a "teaching principal" or a "principal teacher"—in either case subject to annual affirmation or nonrenewal by the faculty.

- Subject schools, on an annual basis, to an external, curriculum-based evaluation, focusing on student learning. The results of such an annual assessment would be made public and would serve to inform parents about the quality of each school.

- Allow parents to choose the right schools for their children from all available schools—and make every effort to ensure that this is an informed choice based on accurate information.

- Give the chosen school the authority to require that parents and students who select that school sign a compact outlining mutual obligations vis-à-vis behavior codes, academic performance standards, parental involvement, and teacher and school commitments. Students and parents would have to adhere to this compact in order to continue in that school—or "shop around" for a school that might be a better match.

- Let schools not chosen by parents and students diminish in size. The vacated space could be filled by satellites of more effective schools or by other newly developed schools.

- Schools that were chosen by more parents and students than they could accommodate could "franchise" themselves by expanding into satellites in spaces vacated by other, less effective schools.

- Designate some schools as "full-service schools." These schools would have health and social services for students who need them, case managers, a lower student-to-adult ratio, more counseling services, and other resources that only some children need. They would be staffed by the most experienced and accomplished teachers and would become the "educational intensive-care units" of each district.

- Decide districtwide the per-capita amount of money allowed for each category of students and allow these amounts to vary. For example, students with greater needs would be allotted a higher per-capita funding support than "regular education" students, as would students in full-service schools and students with special educational needs. This would serve as an incentive for schools to seek these students instead of avoiding them.

- The weighted formula for each student would also include a "margin of profit" so that schools that were more successful in increasing student achievement would have more incentives and could engage in profit sharing. Each profit-making school would decide how to use the extra money.

A market-driven system that includes a two-way choice for public schools could offer incentives for everyone, encourage entrepreneurship, lessen the bureaucracy, phase out failing programs, and replicate successful schools. It would be more responsive to students and more conducive to continuous improvement.

This could radically change the very structure of public education by injecting market dynamics into our system, providing for shared accountability, enabling schools to enforce standards, and empowering students and their parents to choose from among all public schools the one best suited to their needs.

Such a two-way choice would mean that accountability would be built in: parents and students would vote with their feet, while public schools would, for the first time, gain the right to actually enforce the academic, behavioral, and parental-involvement standards they set. In a way, public schools would gain the capacity and authority that private schools have had all along.

But whether schools are public or private, they will continue to flounder in the absence of parameters for a common curriculum, performance standards, common assessments, and higher stakes for students. Making public schools more like private ones makes sense largely because the private school model offers greater opportunity to enforce standards—assuming that there actually are high and rigorous standards to enforce. So the issue is more one of "having standards" and "enforcing standards" than of public schools versus private schools.

It would be a grave mistake to privatize or weaken our children's public schools. Voucher plans that have already been tried have increased inequality without making the schools any better. They merely widen the gap between the haves and have-nots. And that is one social experiment our children cannot afford.

Public schools should be overhauled, not abandoned. We can preserve our commitment to universal access to education by introducing into the public sector some of the private and market dynamics that offer greater promise for better results. That includes putting first things first: high standards of conduct and academic rigor. But standards that cannot be enforced are meaningless.

So let's follow common sense and do what the public wants, what teachers have supported all along, and what our students need. Making public schools more like private schools is a way to begin. Along with the other needed changes, this can help increase the chances that more children will learn better.

Adam Urbanski is director of the Teacher Union Reform Network,
or TURN, and president of the Rochester Teachers Association,
an affiliate of the American Federation of Teachers.

Eleven years later there are more charter schools, but they remain a sideshow more than a reform. As a practical matter all charter school leaders are escapists. They understandably care more about their schools and children than the needs of some broader movement. We were naive to think otherwise. A few districts have adopted chartering as a way to create options. To promote scale, foundations have funded the replication of promising school models and management organizations. But these efforts are small—and isolated in the face of school boards' general hostility. For every district that charters schools, 10 are committed to keeping them out. We continue to believe in the economies of common support and local accountability, but the geographically limited school district may have to be replaced with special charter districts. In the meantime, foundations will have to jump-start the support systems most districts withhold from independent charter schools.—MDM, PTH, RL

PUBLISHED JUNE 5, 1996

CHARTER SCHOOLS

Escape or Reform?

[MARC DEAN MILLOT, PAUL T. HILL, & ROBIN LAKE]

The charter school movement, started as a means of escape for small numbers of dissidents, is evolving into an engine of broader reform for public education. The movement is still small, with fewer than 300 of the nation's 85,000 public schools operating under charters that allow public funding and freedom of action in return for accountability for results, but it might soon be strong enough to transform the definition of public education and the ways school districts operate.

Perhaps the most important sign that the charter school movement is maturing from escape to reform is the effort in many states to raise or eliminate the ridiculously low caps on the numbers of charter schools (25 in Massachusetts and Colorado, 100 in all of California). Without arbitrary caps, the numbers of charter schools in any locality would be limited only by the supply of qualified applicants. In some communities, all public schools might eventually be operated by independent groups of teachers, parents, social service agencies, teachers' unions, or independent nonprofits.

This possibility is a long way from the original dreams of the few teachers and parents who just wanted to remove their own schools from the burdens of regulation and school board oversight. Early charter school supporters saw local boards as major impediments to educational innovation. They wanted to make it easy, almost automatic, for private groups to get charters. The law in Michigan, for example, makes it possible for school sponsors to bypass local boards entirely, by requesting charters from other public agencies, including state colleges and universities.

The possibility of unlimited numbers of charter schools puts a different light on the desirability of automatic approval and multiple routes of authorization. If charters are to become widespread or universal, some mechanism of community oversight is necessary. Charter schools will not be isolated exceptions—they will be the way that the community educates many or all of its children. Some community forum or agent must ensure that there is a school for every student, that parents get help validating schools' claims, and that there is some connection between what students are taught at one level of education (for example, elementary school) and what the next-higher level of education requires. If they are seen as normal ways of delivering public education, charter schools are not about total autonomy. They are about educational diversity, innovation, responsiveness to community needs, and ultimately, improved performance.

Those who, like the present authors, see charter schools as a route to comprehensive reform of public education are critical of local school boards as they now operate. But they think boards need to be reformed into the kinds of community agencies described above, not bypassed entirely. They want charter school laws to transform local boards from operators of a highly regulated bureaucracy into managers of a system of individual schools, each with its own mission, clientele, and basis of accountability.

Supporters of reform-oriented charter school laws do not want to go back to the system of bureaucratic control that led to the charter movement in the first place. They want to create a system of charter schools that takes account of both the public and the private interests in schooling. Charter bills now being drafted in several states would change the powers of local school boards so they can and must authorize charter schools. They would constrain local boards' discretion so that a charter must be granted to any group that can meet established criteria. Once a charter is granted, a school's survival would depend on whether the parents and teachers who run it deliver the kinds of instruction promised and whether, on objective measures, students are learning. Private interests, as represented by parent choice, would count too. Parents could choose among schools, and no school could survive without students. But, again representing a balance of the public and private interests in education, a charter school where students were not learning could be shut down whether or not parents were happy.

No one entirely trusts today's local school boards to give charter applicants a fair chance. Both the "escape" and the "reform" theories of charter schools call for charter applicants to have recourse to appeal if a local board turns down an application. The difference is that the escape-oriented statutes try to set up appeal venues that have biases toward approval of all charter applications, letting a potential school provider shop for an authorizer that is sympathetic with its proposal. Reform-oriented statutes now being drafted would constrain a local board's discretion so that a charter must be granted to any group that can meet established criteria—and cannot be granted to any applicant that fails to meet them.

A move toward objective criteria protects qualified applicants from local boards that would deny charters merely to avoid competition, even while it protects the public from unqualified charter providers. Charter schools could therefore be trusted to claim increasingly large shares of public school students and funding. Some local boards might eventually oversee all-charter systems. Then local boards would no longer operate schools themselves.

They would be more like the Federal Communications and Securities and Exchange Commissions, which promote fair competition and protect consumers, than like an armed service or police department, which runs everything directly.

In their haste to be free of school districts and to establish their own schools, followers of the escape theory of charter schools give up an important source of financial and administrative support. Without some external support, charter schools must provide for themselves all the protections once provided by the district, including start-up capital, liability insurance and teacher retirement, legal advice, and other professional services. As some charter school operators have already found, skimping on assistance and advice puts the whole enterprise at risk, including children's educational opportunities, the founders' own time and money, and the public's funds. Total autonomy is an illusion. Even well-established independent schools join associations to provide access to teacher labor markets, staff development, performance assessment, and help with self-evaluation.

If they are to become central to a whole community's effort to educate its children, charter schools must have clear and reliable relationships with community agencies that can authorize charters, guarantee funding, and hold school operators to their promises. Those community agencies—which for want of a better term we call local school boards—are as essential to a charter-based reform of public education as are the groups of teachers, parents, and others who agree to accept charters to operate individual schools. If the local mix of schools depends entirely on individual initiative, no one is responsible for the overall quality and appropriateness of a community's schools. This consequence is scarcely different from the results of a voucher scheme, under which schools are provided only by private entrepreneurs.

All charter school supporters agree that charter schools should be run by their own founders and staff, and freed from most of the process requirements that limit how current public schools hire and teach. But it matters whether charter schooling is about escape or reform. If charter schools are for escape, charter laws should make it easy for new schools to form without prior community scrutiny of school plans or operators' qualifications, enroll students, and claim public funds. Charter schools' survival should depend almost exclusively on parent satisfaction; no elected board or appointed superintendent should have any discretion about the establishment, continuation, or closing of a charter school.

But if charter schools are for reform, we must devise a system of public education that combines the educational advantages of school independence with the economic advantages of school districts. Today, local school boards are a problem for all charter school applicants. But in the long run, local boards with new missions and limitations can be integral parts of the charter school movement.

Marc Dean Millot has been a senior social scientist at the RAND Corporation, chief operating officer of New American Schools, founding CEO of a K-12 investment fund, and president of a national charter school organization. He founded K-12Network.com in 2003 and edits its Web-based trade publications, *New Education Economy* and *K-12Leads and Youth Services Markets Report,* as well as the podcast School Improvement Industry Week Online.

Paul T. Hill is research professor at the University of Washington's Daniel J. Evans School of Public Affairs. He directs the Center on Reinventing Public Education and is a nonresident senior fellow in the Brookings Institution's Economic Studies Program.

Robin Lake directs the National Charter School Research Project at the Center on Reinventing Public Education. She has authored numerous studies and technical assistance reports on charter schools and, with Paul Hill, co-edited "Hopes, Fears, and Reality: A Balanced Look at American Charter Schools in 2006," the research project's second annual report on charter schools.

Fifteen years later, for-profit schools have not transformed American education. Whittle's Edison Project first promised to run schools at less than the average public school cost, and when that proved impossible, to manage schools more effectively. After millions of dollars of investment, much of it unrecovered, and contracts gained and lost in a number of cities, Edison has produced schools of variable quality, no more successful than the range of public schools. The moral of the story, I believe, is that governance is not what matters for education, and privatization is not a silver bullet. What matters for all schools, regardless of sector, is the quality of teachers and leaders, the richness of the curriculum, and supports for student and teacher learning.—LDH

PUBLISHED OCTOBER 7, 1992

FOR-PROFIT SCHOOLING

Where's the Public Good?

[LINDA DARLING-HAMMOND]

Whittle Communications has made headlines and hopes to make history by creating a chain of for-profit schools that will show up the public education system, as well as private nonprofit schools, by offering a "better product." With promises of high technology to allow for fewer teachers and lower costs, the Edison Project intends to design and operate schools at the nation's average per-pupil cost while making profits.

Many have applauded this bold move, arguing that the effort could shake up sluggish school systems, demonstrate new methods of teaching, and help solve the problems that plague American education. The shock waves may indeed send a wake-up signal to any school systems yet unconvinced that major restructuring of schools is needed. But as a for-profit venture that will pit profits against services for children, the Edison Project will not solve America's real educational problems. At every step of the way the schools will have to decide what educational benefits for students will be forgone in order to ensure adequate profit margins and whether students will be denied admission or underserved because their needs are too expensive to meet. (Although the Edison folks have claimed that any and all students will be admitted, it is difficult to see how the handicapped, those who do not speak English, or those who have other special needs can be well served at the cost targets Whittle proposes.)

There are no good, ethical answers to these questions. Pursuing profits while pursuing the public's broader goals for children's education creates a clear and unavoidable conflict of interest. The record of other for-profit schooling enterprises, such as profit-making proprietary schools and for-profit day-care centers, is not encouraging. A recent study by Sharon Kagan and James Newton of over 400 child-care centers confirmed what smaller-scale studies have found: profits for adults come at a cost to children. On average, for-profit day-care centers provide fewer staff members; lower levels of health, counseling, and other related services to children and families; fewer and less creative materials; less-child-sensitive environments; fewer opportunities for parent participation; and less racial integration than public or private nonprofit centers.

Like these enterprises, the Whittle project will have to decide which services can be reduced or eliminated and which students will be served or not, as profit margins are maintained. The only way to imagine dealing with these dilemmas with any integrity is to structure the task so that they are largely avoided. In fact, the announced plan is to locate most Edison schools in affluent communities such as Greenwich, Connecticut, where home and community supports for education are already well funded and educationally needy students are few and far between. This strategy may allow some interesting new schools to enter the margins of the educational marketplace, but it also makes the Edison Project irrelevant to the major task of American education reform.

Aside from the obvious fact that places like Greenwich are not the communities in which existing public or private nonprofit schools are faltering badly, the real issue is how to create new models of schools that will effectively serve all the nation's children. Even if Whittle finds an attractive package of services to sell to parents whose children are already well along the road to the top of the educational heap, these schools will not answer the important question facing American education: how to educate the world's most diverse group of students, including a record number of immigrants from all around the globe, to the high standards of educational performance required for success in the complex, technological world we now inhabit. Such a task has never before been attempted or achieved for all citizens, beyond a small elite. At this point in history, however, no lesser accomplishment will suffice.

What for-profit schooling does not acknowledge is that education is a public good, not a private commodity. We require all students to attend school so that they will be prepared to participate effectively in the political, social, and economic life of our country. The public welfare—not just the individual's pocketbook—is served when young people become productive, responsible citizens. Our collective failure to create a large-enough number of schools that can achieve these goals for students in inner cities and poor rural areas, for students who are handicapped, for those who do not arrive speaking English, and for racial and ethnic minorities who have traditionally been excluded and underserved by schools is the problem we must solve to survive as a great nation in the 21st century.

There are a great many states, localities, and school-reform networks that are tackling these more fundamental and difficult problems. Major school-restructuring initiatives in states like New York, Vermont, California, Washington, Kentucky, and Georgia are incorporating the lessons of reforms that have succeeded in central cities and poor rural schools with students who are usually written off by traditional schooling—and will be ignored by the Whittle project as well. Theodore Sizer's Coalition of Essential Schools, James Comer's School Development Program, Howard Gardner's Project Zero, Impact II's Teacher Innovation Network—these and other initiatives have already created new models of schooling producing dramatic successes for students in New York City; New Haven, Connecticut; Indianapolis; Louisville, Kentucky; rural Georgia; San Diego; and elsewhere.

These efforts do not reap profits for entrepreneurs, but they reap enormous benefits for all American citizens, including people who may feel themselves to be far removed from the children and parents who are directly served. When central-city high schools graduate all of their students and send most of them on to college, as these "break the mold" schools are able to do, everyone wins: other students, whose aspirations are lifted; local communities, whose streets are filled with more determination and less despair; and citizens everywhere, who pay lower bills for welfare and prison cells while their Social Security receipts are secured by a greater number of young people entering the workforce as productive taxpayers rather than tax users.

Of course the Edison Project, which is looking at these innovative public schools for ideas to build on, may capitalize on what has already been learned. The project certainly has enormous start-up capital and will seek to raise much more, from corporations and other private sources and, with hoped-for vouchers, from the public sector. The real costs thus will be higher than the price that is charged. Unfortunately much of this capital is likely to come from the same sources that might otherwise be supporting school reforms now going on in the trenches—efforts that are less visible and well supported, that are jeopardized by recent education-budget cuts almost everywhere, and that are more essential to the hard work of serious educational change.

The question the American public should ask as it continues to search for bold new ways to redesign our schools is, Where's the public good? As we discover affirmative answers in the efforts of school reformers who work on behalf of children most in need, we should make sure our investments follow. The real bottom line is that when all our children are well educated, the entire nation will profit.

Linda Darling-Hammond is Charles E. Ducommun Professor of Education at Stanford University, where she has served as faculty sponsor for the Stanford Teacher Education Program and launched the School Redesign Network and the Stanford Educational Leadership Institute. She is author or editor of 13 books, including her latest, *Powerful Teacher Education: Lessons from Exemplary Programs* (Jossey-Bass, 2006).

Under the new pressures for high test scores, standards, and labeling schools as failing, this essay is more relevant than it was almost a decade ago. While it is not clear that schools are made better through competition with other schools, it is clear that educators, without shame, need to know how to market what they do and to demonstrate a level of caring for children and families that was barely thought of years ago.—DR

PUBLISHED MAY 19, 1999

COMPETING FOR OUR CLIENTS

[DOROTHY RICH]

Public schools no longer have a built-in, zoned-in public. Schools have to win their clients, their students, the hard way. The charters are coming and so are the vouchers. We can't just say that they will go away. They may run their course, but not until the test scores come in—a few years down the way.

So what do we do in the meantime? We can't run and hide. My recommendation is that we get out in front and compete with these education attractions. It can be a lot easier than we might think.

For example, one of the attractions of charters and vouchers is the promise they seem to hold of more personal attention. This is a major new force in education. We work with parents and community today not simply because the research says this is the way to raise achievement. We do it because these are our clients, and they expect a level of personal service that parents in the past did not. Some parental expectations may be too high, of course, even unrealistic, but to dismiss them out of hand or to fail to work with parents to understand limits and possibilities would be foolhardy in a consumer age.

The impact of a consumer culture, coupled with real worries parents have about education, demands that schools begin to market themselves as businesses do. Is this demeaning? Crass? Degrading? I don't think so.

One of the basic questions I ask in the training programs I conduct is this: In two or three sentences, why would parents want to send their child to your school? If people have trouble answering this, they may well have trouble keeping their schools open.

It's certainly time that schools paid more attention to parents and children as customers. This doesn't mean bowing and scraping to make their every demand a reality. But it does mean making our schools more appealing. We have to pay attention.

This is a message increasingly understood by districts across the country. A principal quoted in the Fort Myers, Florida, *News-Press* this year on that city's new public-school-choice program put it this way: "We're selling our programs and organization, which would be similar to what a businessman would do. I think students will see us as a viable option for learning. It's really a matter of, if we're not pulling in the kids, then we have to work harder."

Parents have concerns beyond academics for their younger children. Transportation is an issue. They want schools close to home so that their kids are not bused across town. They want their children to be with the classmates they have known in earlier grades. Some parents may even move their children from school to school until they get what they perceive to be the right fit.

When parents opt out of the system in favor of different schools, what are they looking for? They are seeking standards, achievement, and high expectations, to be sure. But they are also seeking something more. Here's a quick summary of what I hear from parents across the nation:

- They are seeking some greater form of personal control, some sense that they can express their consumer activism on behalf of their children.

- They are seeking a code of behavior and standards and expectations about how children should act in school.

- They are seeking a school atmosphere that rewards high standards of achievement and behavior and provides disincentives to out-of-control and disruptive students.

- They are seeking a sense that achievement by their children can mean something—that when their children work hard, they will be rewarded.

- They are seeking a sense of greater personal attention—that the school cares about their child, their home, and them.

These realistic expectations deserve to be met. They are not pie in the sky. Public schools that dismiss the message that charters and vouchers are sending do it at their peril. It is a useful message, a reminder we need. And public schools, with their resources and experience, are actually in a stronger position to meet these expectations than start-up schools.

Many parents, in fact, talk about alternatives to the public schools without really knowing what is involved, what benefits they may realistically expect, what pitfalls they may face. We need to provide them with information and leadership. One relatively easy way to do this is to clip, save, and distribute all relevant articles and studies on alternative forms of education. Giving parents all the facts, and not just about the school trying to keep them, can be very persuasive.

When businesses woo customers, they assess their products and services and take steps to make them stronger. Schools can do even better. Here are examples of the kinds of questions school personnel need to ask themselves. Call it a personal school report card:

- Do we know what our customers want? Do we care?

- Are we ready to provide the kind of service and outreach it takes to woo and win our customers?

- Do we have ways (such as surveys) to find out what our customers care about? Do we do this regularly?

- Do we have a written statement of services and written materials soliciting parent comments?

- Do we make strong efforts to inform our customers about issues in education and the pros and cons of various initiatives?

- Do we give our customers the benefit of our expertise? When we buy cars or cosmetics, there are consumer reports to check. Whom do parents ask about schooling issues?

- Do we have frontline personnel trained and assigned to respond effectively to parent questions? This includes administrators, teachers, guidance counselors, and front-office support staff.

- What staff training needs to be provided? What parent training?

- Do employees in all facets of the school's work know how to put across the school's philosophy? Do they know and believe in the basic message and the pluses of our school?

- Do we have a way to determine how well the message is getting through and the effectiveness of our service system? When parents say they are moving their children from our school, is there a sign-out process that helps determine why they are making this change?

- How do I rank the overall service provided at the school where I teach? At the school where my children are enrolled? At the school I wish they could attend? What changes would I make to ensure that my school received more positive answers on this questionnaire?

Just as in the business world, there will always be the unappeasable, unpersuadable school client who can never be satisfied. But when educators get more *yes* answers than *no*'s and *not sure*'s on this modest survey, they will be well on the way to competing effectively for their parents and students.

Dorothy Rich, founder and president of the Home and School Institute, now heads Dorothy Rich Associates. She is author and developer of the MegaSkills Programs. Her next book, *Teachers Need Encouragement, Too,* is set for publication in 2007. She can be reached at www.megaskills.org and by e-mail at dorothyrich@starpower.net.

PART NINE

INSPIRING
LEADERSHIP

We must do more to make sure education meets the needs of our children and the demands of the future. First and foremost, we must continue to hold students, teachers, and schools to the highest standards. We must ensure students can demonstrate competence to be promoted and to graduate. Teachers must also demonstrate competence, and we should be prepared to reward the best ones, and remove those who don't measure up, fairly and expeditiously.—Bill Clinton, *Between Hope and History* (Random House, 1996), p. 44

PUBLISHED SEPTEMBER 10, 1986

SCHOOLS MUST RECONNECT PUPILS, CULTIVATE LEADERSHIP FOR CHANGE

[BILL CLINTON]

Ever since *A Nation at Risk* was issued in 1983, I've been plagued by the nightmare that education reform will go the way of the Hula Hoop, the Twist, and the Edsel. It's awfully hard to keep Americans thinking about something that doesn't lead to easy resolution, something that takes a long time to do thoroughly. In looking at the problems we have now in many states, particularly in the American heartland, it's easy to see how people could become discouraged in their efforts to deal with education problems. So many things need to be done; it's tempting to say, "We've made some progress in education in the last few years; let's move on to other pressing areas."

That would be a mistake. As a governor and as the new chairman of the Education Commission of the States (ECS), I am keeping education at the top of my priority list because I think we have started something that we have to finish. The education reform movement of the early 1980s was not a fad. It was a response to social and economic forces that continue to transform the world around us. The reasons we must radically improve our education system are more compelling now than they were then.

Remember the reasons that lay behind the reforms triggered by *A Nation at Risk, Action for Excellence,* and other reform reports:

• Our economic survival depends on having a stronger education system. That is even truer today. In the last five years, 40 percent of the American people have suffered a decline in their real incomes. Why? Because we were dragged kicking and screaming into worldwide economic competition and we weren't ready. If 4 Americans in 10 are going backwards in terms of real income, we are headed for deep trouble. Our greatest resource is our children's minds; our best hope for dealing with the changes in our economy is to cultivate those minds far more productively than we have had to in the past.

• We also began reform because we thought schools could do better. And we have made significant improvements in many states. People are clearly trying harder, even in these difficult times. But four or five years of incremental improvement is not sufficient.

• We began our reform initiatives in the name of all our children. It has become clear, however, that we are still not addressing the needs of all children. Even when schools have gotten better, too many children remain unaffected. Too many students move out of grade school without basic skills; too many fall prey to teenage pregnancy, alcohol, and drug abuse. Too many students are failing, too many are coasting, and too many are dropping out.

What I want to do first and foremost in the coming year as ECS chairman is to focus on what we can do to "reconnect" those youths who are now disconnected from school, family, the workplace, and the values and skills they need to become productive adults. We simply cannot accept a system that is so unproductive and so inhumane as to let as much as a third, and in some places a majority, of students drop away before receiving their degrees.

What can we do to make our bucket less leaky, to hold out the promise of education to people for whom it appears totally irrelevant, for whom all of our efforts are still failures? If we don't answer this question, I don't think anything else we do to improve schools will work in the long run.

The intelligence is there to be tapped. Where cynicism about "the system" stands in the way, we must find ways to counter cynicism with promise. Where lack of motivation stands in the way, we must find ways—undoubtedly working with people throughout the community—to motivate young people. Where emotional and family problems stand in the way of learning, we must find ways to mobilize community resources and harmonize them so that learning can begin.

The only way I know to deal with these kinds of problems is an old-fashioned way: one-on-one. South Carolina and Texas have some innovative early-schooling programs that bring more one-on-one possibilities into the schools. Let's study them and share our knowledge. In Arkansas, we are requiring each school district to develop an individualized education program for every child whose test scores place him or her below grade level. Other states are looking for ways to further individualize the attention so many students need.

We all need to publicize what works and share it. We may not all be able to reach a dropout rate of 5 percent, but I think every state can reach a dropout rate of 10 percent to 12 percent. We can't do it alone, of course; we will need to work with all of the other agencies that help youth in our states.

The second major issue I want to focus on is related closely to the first: How do we build alliances for change at the school level? I don't think there is any question about the need to restructure the schools. The Holmes Group, the American Federation of Teachers, the Carnegie Forum on Education and the Economy, the ECS, and many other groups are in agreement that the kinds of changes that must take place are structural, not cosmetic.

But what exactly does *restructuring* mean? It means building working partnerships that unleash people's creative energy in a way that makes them free to do their best. It means more involvement of teachers in decisions that affect their daily lives. It means less trivial, meaningless work for teachers and more professional responsibility. It means more involvement of principals in leading people, less in managing the status quo.

Restructuring means, above all, cultivating a leadership for change. The leadership will have to come from all quarters. We need parents, school board members, and teachers willing to take the lead. We need governors continuing to lead as forcefully as they have in the last decade. We need legislators sticking their necks out for change in education, taking risks, and empowering the people closest to the problems to come up with innovative solutions. And we need vigorous new kinds of leadership in our principals and superintendents across the country.

Some months ago I chaired a task force for the National Governors Association on educational leadership and management. The testimony I heard at our meetings opened my eyes. I learned that districts often fail to set priorities for principals and that, as a result, principals spend most of their time managing things—"doing things right" instead of "doing the right things." I learned that many principals find their jobs characterized primarily by fragmentation, their interactions characterized by brevity and incoherence. Most teachers do not see their principals as leaders and do not receive from their principals helpful advice, feedback, or assistance about instruction or curriculum. I learned that the way we use time in schools, the way we have organized staff roles, the way we have structured the curriculum and distributed the authority within schools all constrain the kinds of activities that so many of us now want to see going on in the classroom.

So we're going to have to change the way we train principals and administrators. We're going to have to change the way we use time and staff in schools, the way we structure activities.

It's equally clear to me that state policy can encourage or frustrate leadership. We are going to have to look to the policy community to provide the incentives, the support, and the resources necessary to generate the kinds of leadership for change that are necessary. We are going to need more dialogue between legislators, state and local board members, superintendents, college of education faculty members, principals, teachers, parents, and community groups about what it is we want from our schools and how we are going to collaborate to get it.

We're going to have to take a hard look at certification requirements, the education of administrators, and the evaluation of administrative performance. We're going to have to find ways to reward principals and entire schools for their performance. And when we find the high-performing schools and principals, we're going to have to give them the publicity they deserve.

Much of what we have been doing in education reform has been in response to demands from outside the education system. Often education leaders have been forced into defensive action. The time has come to look upon radical reform in a more positive light, to build a process that promotes continuing reform within the system. After all, reform is what this country has always been about.

The time has come to embrace the challenges of an exciting, if complex and frustrating, time in our lives. The call for new leadership for change is not simply a call for new kinds of administrators. It is a call to take charge of the changes that are upon us and guide them productively toward the ends we all have in view: a sounder, more enabling, more responsible education for all.

When he wrote this piece, Bill Clinton was governor of the state of Arkansas, chairman of the Education Commission of the States, and chairman of the National Governors Association. He went on to serve two terms as president of the United States and is founder of the William J. Clinton Foundation, which promotes global health, economic, and citizen service initiatives.

One quality I would add to my list of long ago is the ability to solve problems creatively. In a way, this connects with imagination. I would encourage search committees to present candidates with moral, ethical, and personnel problems and ask that they come up with creative solutions.—AB

PUBLISHED OCTOBER 13, 1982

OLD QUESTIONS WILL PRODUCE OLD ANSWERS TO THE PROBLEM OF EDUCATION LEADERSHIP

[ALLEN BERGER]

I am heartened these days by the number of positions open for leaders of educational institutions. If a hundred people apply for each position (even with some people applying for more than one opening) and if the best person is picked in each instance, better days for educational leadership are surely on the way.

Yet at the same time that this abundance offers reason for optimism, I think there is also some reason for concern. I don't believe we have grasped what qualities transform educational administration into educational leadership. I am concerned about the qualifications we do not require of candidates for the top jobs in schools and universities. For example, I have yet to read an advertisement for a school superintendency, university presidency, deanship, or principalship that asks candidates to at least demonstrate all, or even many, of the following characteristics: imagination, intelligence, scholarship, compassion, honesty, courage, business and legal acumen, health, humor, magnanimity, as well as the usual requirements such as demonstrated administrative experience. Certainly this is not a complete list; but these qualities are necessary supplements to the traditional skills we associate with the capacity to hold a position of trust and leadership. Why are such qualities important?

Imagination. The function of a school or university is to impart knowledge imaginatively, Alfred North Whitehead reminded us more than a half century ago. The more imaginative power a leader has, the more he or she is prepared for troubled times. In contrast to the person who is crisis bound, the imaginative leader foresees change and prepares accordingly.

Intelligence. The leader must be a thinker who can help students—the technicians of learning—become thinkers ready to prepare for any vocation or profession. To make trenchant, incisive decisions, a school leader must possess broad knowledge, deep understanding, and a high level of adaptability.

Scholarship. Schools and universities serve society by producing and disseminating imaginative, intelligent scholarship. Since an educational leader sets the tone of the workplace, the leader who values scholarship sets an example that will be emulated—scholarship will be produced and, depending upon the reward system, disseminated. Students from all walks of life will respect its value, and the climate of classrooms will reflect their renewed respect. Whatever vocation students choose, they will become lifelong learners and responsible citizens.

Compassion. People who have risen to the heights of their fields of endeavor often cite the importance of having had concerned teachers in their lives. If an educational leader pays only lip service to teaching, the faculty, staff, students, and future generations will suffer the consequences.

Honesty. The hallmark of a school or university is honest intellectual freedom. A leader in education, like leaders in business, must encourage open exchanges of ideas among faculty members, students, staff members, and administrators.

Courage. Honesty without courage results in stagnation. It takes a great deal of courage to act (and to permit others to act) sincerely and truthfully. Does the candidate sway in the political winds? Does he or she have the courage to say and do what is in the best interests of the people he or she represents?

Business and legal acumen. In these economic times, it is imperative that a school or university leader have a broad understanding of what ideas, techniques, and actions common to the business and legal worlds are applicable and, just as important, not applicable to education. Overlooking ideas from business can be as expensive as accepting them blindly. Acceding to legal arguments without question can be as foolish as being oblivious to legalities altogether.

Magnanimity. The leader must be able to cope with small failures—his or her own and those of others—and be large enough in spirit to point the way to new successes that will reflect well on the faculty, the students, and the institution.

Health. Clearly, as in so many other aspects of life, physical well-being and stamina are vital to providing vigorous direction.

Humor. Tempering the serious side of education with a touch of humor fosters mental and emotional balance throughout the trials of tenure in office.

How can these qualifications be assessed in a candidate for a leadership position in education? Easily and simply. Search committees need only ask the appropriate questions. For example, ask the candidate what he or she has read recently. If the answer is, "I've been too busy," you will know right away that he or she does not value reading and does not know how to manage time and delegate tasks properly. Ask the candidate what he or she has written lately; ask to read his or her writing, and ask to read the reviews! (One of the gravest errors in education is to appraise the quantity rather than the quality of the writing of a candidate for a position or promotion.)

I would ask other questions that, admittedly, reflect my own biases: Is the candidate willing to accept a salary lower than that of the highest-paid master teacher or professor? Will arrangements be made for incoming monies to be deposited daily? Will a recycling process for paper and nonpaper products be established if one does not already exist? The candidate's answers to these questions reveal his or her appreciation of the significance of teaching and of faculty and staff members, the value of interest on deposits, and the amount of personal and professional energy the candidate is willing to invest in the job for the sake of the institution.

I also would ask, What does the candidate do for fun and to maintain optimal physical and emotional well-being? Will the prospective leader encourage an annual review of his of her performance by the same people whose performance he or she reviews annually? Does the candidate know how to conduct productive faculty and staff meetings that do not extend beyond an established length of time? Does he or she understand that burnout is merely another word for boredom and that productivity, the opposite side of the coin, can be enhanced by establishing and fostering a challenging, creative—in a word, educational—environment?

These days we have the opportunity to select great leaders at all levels of education. To do so, though, we need to supplement old qualifications and questions with new ones. These are new times. Past experience doesn't predict future performance. The "demonstrated administrative experience" cited by advertisements is not enough; such experience doesn't signify that a candidate possesses the skills and attitudes necessary to meet new challenges. If we continue to ask only the old questions, we will get what we ask for: tired academic administrators who take no responsibility for crises even though they could have been foreseen and prevented. Teachers and students deserve better.

Allen Berger is professor emeritus and Heckert Professor of Reading and Writing (1988–2006) at Miami University in Oxford, Ohio. He received the College Reading Association's Laureate Award for 2005 and is author of approximately 400 articles on reading and writing education.

Predictions in 1996 that more than half of New York State's school superintendents would retire during the next decade proved to be accurate. So did predictions of a shrinking candidate pool to replace the retirees. The combination of these two developments, however, far from resulting in a "crisis" in education, proved to be serendipitous for women. When competition for top jobs declined, women who were hired "by default" opened doors (and eyes) with their competence. In 1996, only 10 percent of New York's superintendents were women. Today they comprise 27 percent. Who would have guessed that the simple marketplace rule of supply and demand would have the greatest impact on gender equity in education?—ST

PUBLISHED OCTOBER 30, 1996

POOLING OUR RESOURCES

[SUZANNE TINGLEY]

So nobody wants to be a school superintendent anymore. According to a new report sponsored by the New York State Council of School Superintendents, "Across the nation, there is a growing concern about the size and quality of the pool of candidates seeking administrative positions." The study's author, Raymond O'Connell of the State University of New York at Albany, explains that "the candidate pool is suffering from an increasing trend toward retirement among current administrators at the same time that fewer professionals are seeking to move into the administrative ranks."

This situation, the professor concludes, portends a "significant crisis for those who believe that high-quality administrators are necessary for the success of today's public schools."

These findings from *A Report of the Status of the Administrative Candidate Pool in New York State—1995,* come as no surprise to some of us in the field. In the education-administration courses I teach for a local university, few if any of my interns aspire to line jobs. Instead, they hope to become department chairs, coordinators, directors—jobs that often require no direct accountability to parents, students, or boards of education. In addition to this removal from the firing line, many currently serving in these quasi-administrative positions still enjoy the classroom teacher's benefits, including tenure and school vacations.

Moreover, administrative positions no longer guarantee significantly higher salaries. Increases in teachers' salaries over the past 10 years have significantly narrowed the gap between teachers and administrators; in some cases, teachers may even lose money by going into administration. When I was a building principal, I actually made less than several veteran teachers in my building. Now, as a superintendent, on a strictly per diem basis I make just slightly more than some experienced teachers in the district who work only 180 days.

The report points to other factors that make administration in general and the superintendency in particular unappealing to prospective candidates. In addition to salary issues, concerns about job security, about the difficulty of satisfying various interest groups, and about increasing criticism of school leadership are cited. These generalizations translate specifically into worries about budget votes, unreliable state aid, union demands, and residency requirements, all of which factor into the dwindling candidate pool.

Well—no one said it would be easy.

But if we step back a moment from O'Connell's more obvious findings, we might approach the apparent dearth of candidates from another angle. Perhaps the pool *is* shrinking if boards are looking for people who look just like all the other candidates they have been hiring over the years. In other words, there may be highly qualified candidates out there—but they may not be white, male, and middle-aged.

Respondents to O'Connell's surveys were primarily district and regional superintendents (most of whom match the above description). They indicated that the candidate pool, especially for the superintendency, has declined in quality and in size. When asked how to improve the situation, according to the report, many suggested mentoring and "reaching out" to women and minorities. However, only about 5 percent of these gatekeepers for district administrative positions indicated that they personally felt a need to change their own recruitment and search processes.

While women have made some inroads to the superintendency, only about 10 percent of the 700-plus superintendents in New York state are women, and the majority of these head up small rural districts. Of the 41 regional superintendencies in the state, two are filled by women. Only six of the nation's 48 largest school districts are headed by women. And although women make up nearly three-quarters of the elementary and secondary teaching corps in this country, only 10 percent of superintendents nationwide are female.

Despite lip service rendered at the state and national levels about encouraging and mentoring potential women candidates for the superintendency, the road to the top district leadership is daunting. Changes at the local level come hard. Boards of education may make public pronouncements about "casting a wide net" for candidates while surreptitiously indicating to their search consultants that they will not seriously entertain women candidates, explaining that "the community" ("parents," "other administrators," "the high school," and so on) isn't ready to accept a woman yet. Consultants, especially those who are paid for the service, deliver what the board wants. According to statistics from *The American School Board Journal,* over half of all board members in 1995 were male, 89 percent were white, and more than 70 percent were 40 years old or older. Successful candidates reflect those demographics.

Ellen Nakashima, writing for the *Washington Post* last April, noted that women who do make it to the interview stage for the superintendency are sometimes "stunned" by questions like, "Does your husband know you're here?" "Can you handle tough discipline problems?" Women candidates report that they are often asked about the impact on their husbands' jobs if they were to move. Worse yet are the brief "courtesy" interviews accorded women candidates by boards or consultants that have already made up their minds about gender but have no valid reason to disqualify a candidate in the first round.

And while mentoring has been recognized by both men and women as key to a potential candidate's success, a good mentor is hard to find. Women mentors are scarce, male mentors are rare. And truth to tell, there are risks involved for the bright, often younger woman who is mentored by a highly visible man. Encouragement for women has more often come from women themselves, through statewide committees and organizations that promote women in administration. But while these groups have served effectively as lobbies, their members unfortunately are generally not gatekeepers for the top jobs in education.

I believe that we will see real changes in the candidate pool and in subsequent hiring practices when searches are conducted under the old classroom rubric: What gets measured gets done. To this I would add a corollary: What gets done gets funded.

We have raised all the consciousness we're going to raise, and we need to move on to develop a plan that includes goals and means to measure progress toward them. The plan needs to have rewards for achieving goals and penalties for ignoring them. Gatekeepers need to be accountable not just to some vague notion of "reaching out" to women and minorities, but to the reality that the report they must file at the end of a search will be scrutinized by the appropriate department of education, and monies coming to a district will depend in some part on its hiring practices.

During the Summer Olympics I listened to a reporter interview the coach of one of the many women's teams that won gold medals for the United States. "To what do you attribute the amazing success of the women's teams?" the reporter asked. "Determination? Training? Hard work?" The coach had a two-word answer: "Title IX." Progress needs to be tied to funding, not to the raised consciousness and goodwill of the gatekeepers.

In 1993, another New York State document, the *Regents Policy Paper and Action Plan for the 1990s,* was published. Entitled "Equal Opportunity for Women," it included several "action strategies" for ending gender discrimination by the year 2000, noting that there were fewer women in education administration now than there had been in the early part of the century.

While the paper clearly identified both goals and strategies, no real penalties were attached for not meeting those goals. The report also noted that the last 20 years have seen the number of women superintendents in New York State increase by 7 percentage points—from roughly 3 percent of the total to roughly 10 percent. At this rate, half the superintendents will be women not in 2000 but in 2136, about 140 years from now.

It is not as if the results of the traditional educational system have been so outstanding that we don't want to tinker with them. In fact, some districts, dissatisfied with school leadership over the years, have turned to private management corporations with varying degrees of success. Clearly we have not drawn educational leadership thus far from the widest ranks of the best and the brightest, and developing opportunities for *all* of the teaching force within the public schools seems to me a systemic change that may result in real improvement.

The superintendency *is* stressful. Employment is precarious, boards are demanding, state aid is random, and voters are unrealistic. But it may be time for the next wave to take on these challenges. *Everyone* into the pool.

Suzanne Tingley is superintendent at Sackets Harbor Central School, Sackets Harbor, New York, and the author of *How to Deal with Difficult Parents* (Cottonwood Press, 2006).

How do districts select and assign principals to schools? Do affluent schools get the plum principal candidates while low-income schools inherit the leftovers? Procedurally, district selection and assignment processes look the same for schools in affluent neighborhoods and those in lower-income neighborhoods. Candidates must hold leadership certification and other professional credentials and progress through a series of interviews and rankings. Still, too many urban schools are saddled with inexperienced and ineffective principals. There seems to be an unspoken code in central offices that Principal A is not good enough for School A but is adequate for School B. How can districts get the better principal in the neediest school?—MCP, LTF

PUBLISHED MARCH 29, 2000

THE PRINCIPALSHIP

Looking for Leaders in a Time of Change

[
MILDRED COLLINS PIERCE &
LESLIE T. FENWICK
]

Years ago, the noted anthropologist Harry F. Wolcott wrote a book called *The Man in the Principal's Office* describing the day-to-day activities of one 1960s-era elementary school principal, Ed Bell. From his morning cup of coffee at home to the final ringing of the school bell in the afternoon, we witness the mundane routines of a schoolman.

History tells us that the past is prologue, or in more colloquial terms, that the more things change, the more they stay the same. Today's public schools and those who lead them may be a lot like those of Principal Bell's day, but at the same time they are quite different.

The student population, for example, is more diverse now than it ever has been. Approximately 36 percent of the nation's students are categorized as members of minority groups (primarily African American or Hispanic). Statisticians predict that by 2004 that figure will increase to 55 percent. In some schools, 90 percent or more of the students speak a first language other than English, often Spanish. Ten percent of the nation's schoolchildren are in special education programs.

While the student population is amazingly diverse, the ranks of the principalship are not. Today's typical principal is a 50-year-old white male who has been a principal for 11 years, works at least 10 hours a day, and plans to retire at 57. Forty years ago, in Bell's day, more than 95 percent of the principals were white males who earned their first appointment at age 35 and worked at least nine hours a day.

In 1961, 31 percent of the teaching force was male, 68 percent was female. Today, more than 73 percent of all teachers are women, and women account for 35 percent of the nation's principals. Remarkably, this increase in the appointment of female principals has occurred only within the past decade or so. In the academic year 1987–88, only 2 percent of principals were female. Despite their representation in the ranks of the teaching force, few were called and few were appointed to school leadership positions.

Only about 13 percent of the nation's principals belong to a minority group. Approximately 11 percent are African American, 4 percent are Hispanic, and less than 1 percent are Asian American. These statistics are especially disturbing when we consider the credentials of those who do ascend to school leadership. African American principals (and teachers) are more likely than their white peers to possess a master's degree and a doctorate. They also come to the principalship with more years of teaching experience than their white peers. Why then their tremendous underrepresentation in the ranks of leadership?

Though significant gains have been made by women, notions about who should lead still tend to support the white male stereotype. In education, typically viewed as America's most level playing field, the leadership remains astonishingly monolithic. Ninety-six percent of the nation's public school superintendents are white males, more than 80 percent of school board presidents and members are white males, and 60 percent of principals are white males.

These statistics prevail despite some striking realities, the foremost being education's long history as a female-dominated field. In addition, African Americans who go on to graduate school are overwhelmingly selected into social science fields, with the highest representation in education doctoral programs. Approximately 60 percent of the doctoral degrees awarded to African Americans are earned in education.

Among the apocalyptic news stories appearing about the schools, the media have begun to proclaim a new problem: the leadership shortage. Across the country, districts are scrambling to fill principal posts.

Several factors have converged to change the landscape of the principalship: (1) increasing ethnic and linguistic diversity of the student population and school communities, (2) decreasing public confidence in the quality of public schools, (3) the press for privatization, (4) increasing school violence, (5–6) waning desirability of the principalship and the concomitantly shrinking pool of principal aspirants, and (7) pressures from the accountability movement to link principals' tenures to students' performance on standardized tests.

The ranks of school leadership are graying and those in the pipeline are either not interested in assuming the top post or have not been cultivated and tapped, as is often the case for female and minority educators. According to a recent study released by the National Association of Elementary School Principals and the National Association of Secondary School Principals, nearly half of urban, suburban, and rural districts, and more than half of elementary, middle, and high schools, reported a shortage of principal candidates. The U.S. Department of Labor estimates that 40 percent of the country's 93,200 principals are nearing retirement, and that the need for school administrators through 2005 will increase by 10 percent to 20 percent.

Approximately 47 percent of the nation's public school teachers have master's degrees. Clearly there is not a dearth of qualified educators. They simply are not seeking the position, preferring instead to acquire seniority in the classroom. Often senior teachers earn more per hour than the principals under whom they serve, when the teachers' 10-month work year and principals' 12-month work year are factored into calculations.

From interviews with superintendents and principals, researchers have concluded that the top three barriers to acquiring sufficient quantity and quality of principals are these: insufficient compensation when compared with responsibilities, the job's generally high stress levels, and the fact that it requires too much time.

Today the school leader is expected to be simultaneously a servant-leader, an organizational and social architect, an educator, a moral agent, a child advocate and social worker, a community activist, and a crisis negotiator—all while raising students' standardized-test performance. Added to these demands is the day-to-day reality of the principalship. The principal must negotiate bureaucratic minutiae, district politics, and community inter-actions. He or she must be able to placate and soothe parents' concerns while also serving as a plant manager who can get the bus schedule right.

It is important that the principal shortage be resolved in ways that pre-serve the role of professional educators as leaders of the schools. We need not look outside the ranks of educators to fill leadership positions in the schools. Many educators are well-qualified. The challenge districts face is to encour-age the able to be willing.

The principalship is not just another job. It is a calling. How do we recruit new leaders for this important work? Where will we find young people willing to be leaders in a place where everyone has an opinion about how you can improve but few regard your work with children as a worthy career choice?

In the final analysis, if we expect exemplary educators to aspire to the principalship, they must be offered more than encouraging platitudes, a slap on the back, and a set of keys.

Mildred Collins Pierce is president of the Fund for Educational Excellence
in Baltimore, Maryland. She is past director of The Principals' Center
at the Harvard Graduate School of Education.

Leslie T. Fenwick is newly appointed dean of the School of Education at
Howard University and a former visiting scholar in education at Harvard University.

[INDEX]

A

Academic achievement: encouragement from teachers and, 3–5;
high-stakes testing and, 185–186;
reading scores and, 75; school
vouchers and, 187

Accessibility of knowledge, 74

Accountability, 52, 66, 79, 167, 168,
195–196, 204

Advanced Placement courses, 3, 4, 65

African Americans: Census 2000 and,
31, 32, 34; cybersegregation and,
105–109; principalship and, 236,
237; racial segregation and, 23, 25,
26, 35, 36–38; racism and, 40–44

Alberts, B., 118

American Federation of Teachers
(AFT), 47, 50, 149, 223

Amrein, A. L., 185, 186

Annenberg Foundation, 10

Anrig, G., 52

Anti-Babel standards, need for, 60–64

Appiah, K. A., 109

Applebee, A., 88, 89

Arts education, neglect of, 90–92

At-risk children, 169–170

B

Baker, E., 145

Bell, E., 235, 236

Bell, T. H., 160, 163

Ben Jelloun, T., 44

Berger, A., 226, 229

Berliner, D. C., 185, 186

Bethune, M. M., 108

Bill and Melinda Gates Foundation,
79, 80

Bishop, J., 76, 77

Black principals, 236, 237

Black students: Census 2000 and, 31,
32, 34; Internet access and, 105–
109; racial segregation and, 23, 25,
26, 35, 36–38; racism and, 40–44

Board of Education, Brown v., 28, 36,
37, 38

Boyer, E. L., 160

Braun, H., 186

Breadth of knowledge, 70, 74

Brown v. Board of Education, 28, 36,
37, 38

Bruner, J., 67

Bugscope program, 118

Bush, G.H.W., 151, 169

Bush, G. W., 155, 186

C

Carnegie Corporation of New York, 10,
15, 16

Carnegie Foundation for the Advancement of Teaching, 121, 144

Carnoy, M., 186

Ceci, S., 164

Census 2000, U.S., 30–34

Cezanne, 91, 92

Education through occupations, 183
Educational leaders: principalship candidates, 235–238; qualities of, 226–229; restructuring and, 168, 221–225; training for, 224; women as, 230–234, 236
Educational research: contradictions in, 185–188; guidelines for, 188–190; policy forum for reviewing, 190–191
Ellington, D., 108
Entrepreneurial system of education, 195–200, 204. *See also* For-profit schooling
Equality of educational opportunity, 23–29
Expert thinking, 124
Extracurricular activities, 81

F

Fallacy of egocentrism, 153
Fallacy of invulnerability, 154
Fallacy of omnipotence, 153
Fallacy of omniscience, 153
Fenwick, L. T., 235, 238
Ferguson, Plessy v., 38
Finn, C. E., Jr., 166, 172
For-profit schooling, 211–214. *See also* Entrepreneurial system of education
Franklin, J. H., 23, 29
Fullan, M., 86

G

Galbraith, J., 9
Gardner, H., 53, 60, 64, 213
Gates, H. L., Jr., 105, 109
Gates Foundation, Bill and Melinda, 79, 80
Geertz, C., 91
Gerstner, L. V., Jr., 11
Gibson, A., 108
Glenn, A., 115
Goals 2000: Educate America Act, 55, 61

Goldberg, W., 8
Goleman, D., 120
Good, H., 3, 5
Goodlad, J. I., 53, 159, 165
Graham, M., 92
Greene, M., 90, 92
Gregorian, V., 10, 16
Grubb, W. N., 179, 184

H

Habits, teaching of, 174–175
Hakim, J., 93, 96
Hanushek, E. A., 186
High schools: comprehensive, 179–183; harder but not better reforms for, 65-69
Highet, G., 135
Hill, P. T., 206, 210
Hirsch, E. D., Jr., 70, 78, 90, 94
Hitler, A., 154
Hodgkinson, H., 30, 34
Honig, B., 171
Horton, M., 43
Hutchins, R. M., 162

I

Iacocca, L., 9
Income and reading scores, 75
Information-technology skills, list of, 125–126
Integrity: defined, 131; teaching, 131–136
Intellectual capabilities and information technology, 126
Internet access: African Americans and, 105–109; edutopia and, 115–122
Iowa Tests of Basic Skills, 72
Isaac, K., 144

J

Job performance and reading scores, 75